AUGUST STRINDBERG

WORLD DRAMATISTS SERIES

First Titles

WORLD DRAMATISTS

AUGUST STRINDBERG

GUNNAR OLLÉN

With halftone illustrations

FREDERICK UNGAR PUBLISHING CO.
NEW YORK

*Translated from the original German
by Peter Tirner
Published by arrangement with Friedrich Verlag,
Velber, Germany*

*Copyright © 1972 by Frederick Ungar
Publishing Co., Inc.
Printed in the United States of America
Library of Congress Catalog Number: 76-153125
Designed by Edith Fowler
ISBN: 0-8044-2664-3 (cloth)*

CONTENTS

CHRONOLOGY

1849   Johan August Strindberg is born in Stockholm on January 22. His father is Carl Oscar
Strindberg, former spice dealer and now a
commission agent; his mother the former
housemaid Ulrika Eleonora Norling.

1853   Strindberg's father goes into bankruptcy.

1867   On May 25, Strindberg graduates from high
school in Stockholm. In the fall, he begins his
studies at Uppsala University.

1868   In the spring, Strindberg works as substitute
teacher in an elementary school; in the fall,
also as private tutor.

1869   In the spring, he interrupts his medical studies; in the fall, he fails dismally as aspiring
actor at the Dramatic Theater. After an un-
successful suicide attempt, he writes, in four
days, his first drama, the two-act *A Name
Day Gift*, rejected by the Dramatic Theater;
the manuscript is lost. At the end of the year,
he writes *The Freethinker*, also rejected.

1870   Early in the year, he writes an outline of
Erik XIV, but later burns the manuscript. In

January he finishes *Declining Hellas*. Resumes studies at Uppsala in the spring. The one-act play *In Rome*, completed at the end of March, gives Strindberg his first stage success, on September 13. In the late summer he re-works the Hellas play into *Hermione*.

1871   Early that year, in a mere two weeks, he re-vises his *Blot-Sven* (1870) into the tragedy *The Outlaw*; the final version is finished in late summer.

1872   In March, Strindberg leaves Uppsala and be-comes a journalist in Stockholm. He finishes the prose version of *Master Olof* on August 8. In November, his second attempt, in Göte-borg, to become an actor fails.

1874   In December, he finds employment as tem-porary assistant at the Royal Library in Stockholm, where he remains until 1882. First revision of *Master Olof*, at the turn of the year.

1875   In the spring, Strindberg meets Captain Wrangel and his wife Siri von Essen.

1876   In May, he finishes a new version of *Master Olof*, this time in verse.

1877   Strindberg finishes *Anno 48* early in the year. On December 30, he marries Siri von Essen (1850-1912) who had meantime been di-vorced.

1880   January 16, he finishes *The Secret of the Guild*.

1882   May 1, finishes *Lucky Per's Journey*, a play commissioned by theater director Ludvig Josephson. In early September, he completes *Sir Bengt's Wife*.

1883   In the fall, journey to France (Grez, Paris).

1884   Around New Year's Day, Strindberg moves to French Switzerland.

1886   *Marauders* finished end of November.

1887   In January, Strindberg moves to Bavaria. On February 15, he finishes the tragedy *The Father*. In June, first stage projects planned jointly with August Lindberg. In the fall, journey to Copenhagen and environs. Toward the end of the year, he revises *Marauders* under the new title *Comrades*.

1888   He completes the naturalistic drama *Miss Julie* in early August. *Creditors* is completed late that summer.

1889   Strindberg finishes the one-act play *The Stronger* on January 2, the one-act *Pariah* on January 9. On February 9, he completes dramatization of his own novel *Hemsö Folk*, and in early March, *Simoom*.

1892   Divorce from Siri von Essen. On February 3, *The Keys of the Kingdom of Heaven* is finished; in March, Strindberg writes *The First Warning* and *Debit and Credit*; he finishes *Facing Death* on April 15, and *Mother-love* in May. In the late summer, Strindberg writes the one-act play *Playing with Fire*, and immediately thereafter (before September 13) *The Link*. In September, he moves to Berlin.

1893   On May 2, on the island of Heligoland, Strindberg marries Frida Uhl (1872-1943).

1894   Frida Uhl leaves Strindberg, in October.

1897   Divorce from Frida Uhl. Another stay in Paris. Publishes *Inferno*, an autobiographical novel.

1898   Strindberg completes *To Damascus, Part I* on

March 6, *To Damascus, Part II* on July 17. *Advent* is finished on December 19.

1899   In February, he finishes the "serious comedy" *There Are Crimes and Crimes*; on April 20, *The Folkung Saga*; in June, *Gustav Vasa;* and in July, *Erik XIV.* In the fall, he returns permanently to Stockholm.

1900   On March 7, Strindberg completes *Gustav Adolf.* On July 26, the "serious comedy" *Midsummer* is finished, and at about the same time he completes *Casper's Shrove Tuesday.* In October and November, he writes *Easter.* About this time Strindberg meets the actress Harriet Bosse. On October 31, he completes the marital drama *The Dance of Death, Part I; Part II* follows in December.

1901   On January 5, *The Bridal Crown* is completed, to be followed end of February by *Swanwhite*, a fairy play which Strindberg, on March 5, dedicates to his bride Harriet as an engagement present. In May, he marries Harriet Bosse (1878-1961). On June 23, *Carl XII* is completed; in July Strindberg writes *To Damascus, Part III*; on September 3, he completes the historical drama *Engelbrekt*, and on September 23, *Christina. A Dream Play* is completed end of November.

1902   On March 16, Strindberg finishes the historical drama *Gustav III*; in July, he abandons *The Hollander*, unfinished.

1903   *The Nightingale in Wittenberg* is finished on September 5. Strindberg continues work on his "world-historical" series with *Moses* in mid-September, *Socrates* in mid-October, and on November 5 he concludes, for the time being, with *Christ*.

1904   Divorce from Harriet Bosse, in November.

1907   February 13 sees the completion of the first chamber play, *The Thunderstorm*; the second, *After the Fire*, is finished in early March, and the third chamber play, *The Ghost Sonata*, on March 8. In the spring, Strindberg works on the fragment *Island of the Dead*, and on June 19 he finishes the fourth chamber play *The Pelican*. On November 26, the Intimate Theater, under the direction of August Falck and August Strindberg, opens with *The Pelican*.

1908   In ten days during August, Strindberg writes the historical drama *The Last Knight*, followed on September 7 by the fairy play *Abu Casem's Slippers* and, on September 23, by *The Regent*, second part of a trilogy begun with *The Last Knight*; the third part, entitled *The Earl of Bjälbo*, is finished that same fall. Toward the end of the year, Strindberg gives dramatic form to "the fantasy" *The Black Glove*.

1909   In the spring, Strindberg writes his last drama, *The Great Highway*.

1910   The Intimate Theater closes its doors on December 11.

1912   May 14: Strindberg dies of cancer of the stomach.

STRINDBERG:
HIS TIME AND HIS WORK

Strindberg possessed extraordinary natural endowments to make him a dramatist: his self-esteem was highly developed, and he was exceedingly impressionable. These two traits are of fundamental importance in judging his work.

Strindberg's concern with his prestige and independence never flagged. His pride was easily injured. As is the case with so many people of strong feelings, his emotions often rose to such a state of turmoil that he could not give them adequate expression in normal conversation. On such occasions, he would abruptly turn his back on the company and mutter incomprehensible threats. Later, in the quiet safety of his meticulous study, the proper repartee would come to his mind; and with the true artist's urge to impose form on life, he would transpose his fury to the fictitious world of the stage.

His impressions were clear and vivid in every detail, and stayed with him throughout his life: his memory was extraordinary. His sensibility afforded him insights into many dramatically fruitful problems of human relations; but it could become a burden even to himself. The world seemed to assail him. Merely to walk down the street was almost as much of an ordeal for him as to appear on stage. The least disruption of his daily routine upset his equilibrium utterly. Even the most common of daily events could give rise to the most uncommon conflicts within him. A man of such temperament obviously had to hide himself from the world.

Life seemed to Strindberg less a struggle of man against himself than a struggle of all against all in mutual self-assertion, or a struggle between man and God. These struggles fascinated him, they involved him deeply—and from his first drama to his last, he never ceased trying to gain clarity about them by throwing a sharp spotlight on their various aspects. His easily injured ego, his feeling that he was oppressed and an outcast—he compensated for both by creating mighty kings and supermen in his plays. He made these fictional characters the spokesmen of his own will to power, and of his knowledge of a superiority, to which his shy temperament and the world around him did not allow full scope.

A housemaid's son, but married to a noblewoman (Siri von Essen), Strindberg was able to conquer his feelings of social inferiority by describing, in the tragedy *Miss Julie* (1888), the decline of the nobility of birth and the survival of the nobility of the mind. In his one-act plays, he who thought himself persecuted by the "small minds" could celebrate triumphant victories of intellectual supermen in the "battle of the brains."

After the agonizing period represented by his autobiographical novel *Inferno*, he needed to compensate for his religious insecurity, his guilt feelings toward God. He showed that all men, not only those laden with guilt, must suffer in order to be reconciled with God. He made himself the champion of suffering mankind, the mediator bargaining with God on the loftiest level. In his visions of Judgment Day—*The Ghost Sonata* and *The Pelican* —the former penitent now stands by the side of his God as a prophet meting out punishment. At the finale of *The Great Highway*, he does not humbly sink to his knees asking the Almighty for His blessing: he requests a friendly favor, without formality, as one of the world's great to another.

Strindberg's sensibility made it inevitable that he should be prone to childlike enthusiasm; but if the objects of his enthusiasm turned out to be inadequate, he felt cruelly disappointed. In order to protect himself from such shocks, he tried to expose as worthless anything that dangerously attracted him: wealth, honor, power, women. His intense awareness of life's duplicity, its alluring appearance and horrid reality, its beauty and ugly darkness, is among the most powerful motives of his dramatic creation.

Encouraged by Ibsen's example, Strindberg turned from a disappointed romantic into a champion of enlightenment. The most famous examples of this shift are *The Father* (1887), in which Strindberg exposes to the world the inferno raging in the heart of a respected and comfortable officer's wife; *The Dance of Death* (1900), which dissects a marriage with such skill that it made Strindberg internationally famous as the demon surgeon of middle-class marriage; the poetic masterpiece *A Dream Play* (1901), in which he showed how life's bright moments always bring dark reversals in their train;

and the chamber plays *The Ghost Sonata* and *The Pelican* (both 1907), in which Strindberg, like God's own executioner, ruthlessly exposed the moral decay of Stockholm's upper classes.

The dominant themes in the love affairs which Strindberg put on stage were the lovers' first enchantment, followed by violent desire, nervous self-consciousness, and hatred. Strindberg's portrayal of the relation between man and woman contains a good deal of yearning for the mother image; it also shows the artist's delight in beauty, as well as his fearfully limited capacity for compassion. The reasons are obvious. A man whose inner life was as stormy as Strindberg's, a man who had to struggle constantly to avoid the hidden reefs of suicide and madness, a man all too complex and self-centered—such a man could never bend to the needs of others, could never find enduring happiness with a woman.

In the scenes of married life which Strindberg put on stage, he offered with ever-varied piquancy a rich mixture of diabolical malice, mutual revulsion and distrust, inconstancy, envy, sadism, and brutality. But there is little selflessness and kindness, tact, or forgiving humor; there is little spontaneous generosity or courtesy, consideration, simple friendliness, or understanding of human foibles. Strindberg made his leading characters respond to others as he himself responded. Love, for him, knows only extremes; it is supremely sweet or supremely bitter.

Strindberg's brutal portraits of marriage have been staged best, and most frequently, by the Germans. The British thought them either disgusting or slightly comical, while the French regarded them as the product of that curious creature known as "the woman-hater of the North."

Yet the intensity of the battle between the sexes Strindbergian style is fascinating. His dialogue caresses, slaps, and crushes. It knows moods of disquieting calm before the storm and of thundering hell, transcending ecstasy and suffocating muck. There is incredible vigor and ruthlessness in his portrayals of the hysterically rapid shift from hot desire to revulsion. The scenes of passionate interplay between two unyielding partners are often embarrassing, but they are dramatically effective.

Three times, Strindberg's love affairs ended in marriage. In each case the woman was a foreigner, and of an independent and artistic nature: Siri von Essen was Finnish and an actress, Frida Uhl was Austrian and a journalist, and Harriet Bosse was a Norwegian and also an actress. They were all three unusual women, and there was about them a touch of the demonic; the dramatist liked women who were strong enough to resist him. As he made Indra's daughter in *A Dream Play* say: "The battle of opposites brings forth strength."

His own love affairs, and most of his dramatic portrayals of love affairs, always went through the same five phases. First, love strikes like lightning; it is "love at first sight." Next, enchanted by his lady's heavenly beauty, the lover sinks to his knees in adoration, and at the same time yearns to be cradled at her breast as if she were his mother. After the beloved has made the first move toward intimacy, he becomes the proud gallant. In the fourth phase, after the lovers' physical union, his feelings of inferiority awaken, and he believes that he has failed to satisfy her. Filled with the suspicion that she holds him in contempt, he now regrets his former gentleness, counterattacks, and begins to humiliate her. Fifth phase: a bitter struggle for domination, consuming jealousy, hatred. Then, when the relationship has collapsed and the lovers are separated, his yearning awakens once more. Now the whole procedure is repeated. The lover is happiest if he sees his beloved only on rare occasions.

Strindberg's religious life, whenever he attempted to give it dramatic form, resembles his relation to women. We never find him immersed in comforting communication with God; on the contrary, he always shows a—conscious or unconscious—yearning for the protection of the Eternal One, conceived as father or as divine mother, together with a pride that revolts against the lack of freedom implied in such protection.

With an incredible intensity and merciless candor, Strindberg turned the spotlight upon the conflicts of his own complicated self. There was high ambition in his endeavor to portray his characters with an almost Shakespearean empathy—to show them three-dimensional, objectively, observed from a distance. He was often superbly successful, almost always so with his minor characters. But on occasion, particularly in his marital dramas, he threw his own personality into the battle and gave wholehearted support to his alter ego, while making a caricature of the opponent. There are touches of monomania in his dramatic self-portraits; but on the whole, the ego he projected so assiduously was rich and varied enough to provide constantly new, dramatically effective material.

Strindberg's plays abound with original and interesting characters; but there are few among them with whom the average public could identify as readily as, say, the women of the 1880s could identify with Ibsen's Nora. Strindberg's extreme characters are the strength as well as the weakness of his dramatic work. Where they lack universal validity, they are fiery and original; they may often be bizarre, but they are never trite. They approach universality most closely when they represent ideas engaged in a struggle for power, as in the great confrontation between Gustav Vasa and Bishop Brask.

By stressing ruthless self-assertion at the expense of humor, kindness, and patience, Strindberg himself limited the general appeal of his plays as compared with those of Ibsen or Shakespeare. On the other hand he was able, with an astuteness that bears the mark of genius, to expose the destructiveness and obduracy of the human animal, and to present it strikingly magnified by the poet's vision. The heroine in *Miss Julie*, the protagonist in *The Father*, the couple in *The Dance of Death*, the siblings in *The Pelican*, and the young student in *The Ghost Sonata*—all come face to face with the law of the jungle in the midst of civilization. These dark perspectives often expand into a pessimistic world view, showing the influence of Schopenhauer's and Eduard von Hartmann's philosophy coupled with the Christian yearning for deliverance. Strindberg became the interpreter of the groaning and travail of creation, the spokesman of that generation which, with dark forebodings, moved toward the era of world wars.

Strindberg often took the cue for his dramatic work from an inner conflict. Something within him ferments or erupts, he becomes enraged, and his own rage becomes his inspiration. He then wrote at breakneck speed, with barely a thought to his public. Such works tended to be of a piece and highly effective, but some of the details and verbal exchanges stemmed so directly from his own immediate surroundings that they seemed obscure and perplexing to those not familiar with their true source. When he was in the throes of inspiration, Strindberg did not always consider how much could be expected of the audience, or keep in mind the technical possibilities of the stage. To him, many of his dramatic visions were wholly personal utterances. Let others look out for themselves in their attempts to understand, or to put on the stage, what he had written!

Strindberg's choice of model may seem at times irrelevant and even mysterious to the spectator. But the literary critic cannot be content with that. The stage director, too, must concern himself with the model Strindberg had in mind for a given character. In casting the role of Queen Christina, for example, it is important to know that Strindberg wrote this splendid role for Harriet Bosse—he had in mind her charming figure, her German descent, her striking mixture of demoniacal beauty and catlike suppleness. In these matters, the playwright departed radically from the historical Christina with her masculine ways and pronounced intellectualism.

It is necessary to find out who Strindberg's models were if we are to refute those irresponsible theories and false symbolic interpretations with which his work soon found itself surrounded. His relation to his models was strikingly ambivalent. Some of them were clearly meant to be recognizable, at least to an inner circle. Strindberg's intention was to punish, or enlighten, those who had modeled for his characters, though to the public they might seem purely fictional.

Even in his most visionary plays, Strindberg remained the investigator. Throughout his life, he retained that love of hard fact which he had developed as a merchant's son and student of nature, and held matters of pure imagination in contempt (though he did at times "lapse" into pure fantasy, as in *Lucky Per's Journey*). He felt that each role gained value and significance in proportion as his material was taken directly from real life. He was a scientific observer and at the same time a psychologist who, under the thin disguise of dramatist, offered astute contributions to the understanding of *homo sapiens*, whether he was dealing with an impulsive young lady of the nobility or an artillery captain celebrating his silver wedding anniversary. In his capacity as scientific observer and historian, he gave us new and revolutionary contributions to the interpretation of such controversial historical figures as Martin Luther and Queen Christina.

At times, his scientific bent proved a hindrance to the creative artist. His blind faith in psychiatry, for example, drove him to draw absurd generalizations from pathological exceptions, and his enthusiasm for genealogical connections is responsible for many dry and tiresome passages in his historical plays. But fortunately for Strindberg the dramatist, his indomitable imagination, relentlessly enlarging, suppressing, or transmuting reality, comes crashing through all his "factual reports."

Strindberg's works contain very few epic longueurs, because his pieces abound with the battles of opposites, precisely as the poet intended, even when

the verbal exchange is among like-minded characters. Every new word, every new statement seems
meant to top all that precedes it. As we turn the
page, we can never predict what the next rejoinder
will be. The originality of his perspectives brings
ever new surprises.

This style leaves its mark on the construction of
individual scenes as well. Strindberg's dialogue, the
dramatic effects of which moved and delighted the
author himself, pierces straight to the heart of reality, more pitilessly and often more sensitively than
Ibsen's (but, in turn, Strindberg's scenes often are
not resolved as smoothly, as logically, as Ibsen's).
Strindberg's drama is difficult to translate into for-
eign languages. His language is impulsive and sweep-
ing, and often hits home like a whiplash, occasionally
skipping a whole train of thought. It is marked by
its vigorous and at the same time amazingly natural
and pointed imagery. Even the most somber lines
shine with the author's delight in happy formulations. Yet for all his stylistic merit at times we encounter phrases that have a wooden, convoluted,
lifeless ring.

The style of Strindberg's verse drama is uneven.
In part, the explanation may be that the author
spent many years away from his native country,
during which time he wrote occasionally in French
or German. But the decisive reason for the uneven-
ness is his impatient work habits: he would attack
his chosen theme in a furious assault, cast it into
dialogue at headlong speed, and then put the result
aside. He seldom troubled to read over what he had
just written, let alone polish or improve upon it.
Corrections in his manuscripts are rare.

This attitude toward his own work is obviously

based on sound instinct. The fast pace of his best pieces gives them a unified, controlled mood. Such great works as *The Father*, *Miss Julie*, and *The Dance of Death* were each written in only a few weeks. The dialogue is knitted together intuitively, as if it had been written as fast as it can be read. If Strindberg did not always write as logically as he spoke (or as he claimed speech ought to be) it was because he had no desire to let his restless poetic rhythms be broken by the trivia of syntax. Strindberg's element is the raging, stormy sea, not the peaceful fountain in the park. The well-groomed minor art forms provoked only his profound contempt.

Strindberg had already achieved international fame with his naturalistic plays on love and marriage when he set out upon a radical renewal of modern drama with his dreamlike plays after *Inferno*. He was more radical than Ibsen. His dream-play technique has had a decided influence upon the drama of symbolism and, in a certain sense, of expressionism as well. That influence can be felt even in the most recent generation of writers, including those of the theater of the absurd. The dissolution of the ego, ambiguity, split personality, dream sequences and transitions, a certain open-endedness, the steady focus on the demoniacal character of existence, violent dislocations of space and time: for all of these revolutionary innovations, the modern theater is indebted to Strindberg.

Strindberg's breakthrough as international dramatist came at the turn of the century, when Emil Schering's translations and Max Reinhardt's staging opened the gates for the high tide of Strindberg plays that flooded the German theater. It reached its peak in the years after World War I, about 1920. In the mid-twenties, interest declined, and by the early thirties Strindberg was almost forgotten, until the end of World War II. But then came a decade of extreme popularity, which reached its peak in 1949, the hundredth anniversary year of Strindberg's birth, and firmly established his position as one of the world's great dramatists. Radio gave his plays a new medium, and several of them seem written to order for the intimate miniature stage of the television studio. The close-up, which allows the camera to show the most subtle changes of mood with little technical apparatus, corresponds exactly to Strindberg's intentions in his intimate drama, whether it be his naturalistic or his dream-play creations.

In our era, when stage, radio, television and the films are hotly competing with one another, and every art form offers its own particular strength, the opportunities to produce Strindberg's dramatic work have become much richer than they were at a time when only the stage was available to him. Strindberg's drama had never been tailored to fit the commercial demands of the theater. Strindberg did write for the theater, and he did see his characters performing under stage lights. But the theater and the stage for which he truly wrote often existed only in the vision of his imagination.

PLAYS

A Name Day Gift
(*En namnsdagsgåva*, 1869)

Strindberg's first play, a comedy in two acts, came to his mind immediately after his dismal failure as a would-be actor at the Dramatic Theater in 1869. It deals with a woman's reconciliation with her stepson. Conflicts in Strindberg's own family furnished the core of the plot: the young man's struggle for his rights turns him against his father; the woman plays the role of the hoped-for conciliator. Strindberg wrote the play in four days. It was submitted to the Dramatic Theater, but rejected. The manuscript was subsequently lost.

The Freethinker
(*Fritänkaren*, 1869)

Immediately upon completion of his first comedy, Strindberg set himself a fresh task. Karl, the young hero of *The Freethinker*, is a typical Strindbergian character, a man who likes to challenge others, an oversensitive idealist with a tendency to seek out intellectual controversy. He is fighting for a "religion of love and truth," because Christ to him is not a god but "the god-sent ideal human being." He rejects with contempt the idea of Christ as the victim who is to be sacrificed to atone for man's sins. Karl, taking his stand for his own faith, breaks with his fellow students at Uppsala who withdraw behind a flood of popular-atheistic verbiage. He gets into a heated conflict with a pietistic and contentious clergyman who asserts that God is the God of Punishment and that the earth is a vale of tears. Karl is forced to break off his engagement to the clergyman's sister, and his "freethinking" also causes a break with his conventional parents and his brother. The play ends as Karl, who has become a schoolteacher, is dismissed for heresy, and plans to emigrate to America, dreamland of freedom. *The Freethinker* lays bare the immorality of conventional Christians, and their revolting intolerance. Behind the banner of religion hides depravity.

A religious debate cast in dialogue form, the little play is the first intimation of Strindberg's dramatic power.

HERMIONE
(1870)

After the Dramatic Theater had declined *The Freethinker* as well, Strindberg tried his hand at an historical play. His search for a theme first took him to classical antiquity, because all things Greek were then in fashion. Thus a three-act play in blank verse came into being under the title *Declining Hellas* (*Det sjunkande Hellas*). In January, he submitted it to the Dramatic Theater, but it was returned. In the late summer of 1870, he reworked it into the five-act *Hermione*.

The play tells of Hermione (in *Declining Hellas*, her name is Antigone), daughter of a high priest, who is sent out to assassinate Philip of Macedonia, whose armies are threatening Athens. Hermione falls in love with Philip and has to pay for it with her life. The piece is essentially a superficial exercise in style.

IN ROME
(*I Rom*, 1870)

After *Hermione*, Strindberg turned to Swedish history with an ambitious tragedy about Erik XIV, but he later burned the manuscript. Instead he produced a brief one-act play telling an episode in the life of the Danish sculptor Thorvaldsen. The hero, residing in Rome during 1803, has just completed his first masterpiece, a statue of Jason; however, he is completely without funds, and is about to abandon his artistic career when at the last moment a rich Englishman turns up and buys the sculpture.

With this one-acter, Strindberg had taken another step forward as a delineator of character. His protagonist seems a product of introspection rather than observation, but Thorvaldsen's friend, the painter Axel Pedersen, a carefree, lively fellow, is a successful portrait. The play's dialogue is considerably more supple and quick than that of the earliest works for the stage. The rapidity of Strindberg's development is astounding, but the drama's structure is technically weak because it lacks a conclusion. The appearance of the English Maecenas merely prompts Thorvaldsen to postpone his return to Copenhagen, but the central question—what is Thorvaldsen's true vocation?—remains unanswered.

The Outlaw
(*Den fredlöse*, 1871)

During his student days in Uppsala, Strindberg became especially fascinated with the world of Icelandic sagas. A literary first fruit was the drama *Blot-Sven* (1870); however, he burned the manuscript a few weeks later. But early in 1871 he rewrote *Blot-Sven*, "in a fortnight," into the one-act play *The Outlaw*, which he further revised at the suggestion of the Dramatic Theater.

The play tells the story of the Earl Thorfinn of Iceland, a hard twelfth-century man who wages a lone battle against Christianity and is punished by God. To gain control of Iceland, Thorfinn brings in warriors from Norway, but almost his entire fleet is destroyed in a storm at sea. Thorfinn himself escapes, but on his return he finds that his daughter Gunlöd has become a convert to Christianity. Outraged, he further learns that he must submit to the judgment of the Icelandic Assembly, which has declared him an outlaw because of acts of pillage committed before he sailed for Norway. His enemies are already surrounding his farmstead. In this hour of need, Thorfinn turns to the God of the Christians. Mortally wounded, he yields to the new faith by blessing his daughter's union with the Christian Gunnar, and dies with the word "God" on his lips.

The dialogue of the play is exceedingly stylized. Its abruptness and rapid execution is in striking harmony with Strindberg's impatient temperament. *The Freethinker* was a reformer who intended to convert people; *The Outlaw*, on the contrary, is himself converted. It is interesting to note the manner in which the Almighty forces the Earl's submission: he employs suffering—in the sense of Strindberg's post-*Inferno* plays—to whip the presumptuous sinner toward the Cross.

Strindberg's often noted hate-love finds its first expression in *The Outlaw*. The play's structure is more thoroughly thought out than that of *In Rome*, but individual scenes are much too abrupt to grip and hold the audience.

Master Olof
(*Mäster Olof*, 1872-77)

Why was it that Strindberg, now free and independent, selected the Swedish reformer Olaus Petri as his central character when next he set out to write a play in the grand manner? One important reason may have been that Swedish history was a genre which was then enjoying great popularity on the nation's stages. Yet the genre made it difficult to obtain friendly treatment from the critics, since the playwright was expected to present contemporary ideas even when the plot itself was set in the remote past. This tendency was especially strong in bourgeois historical drama, a lesser form of literature which enjoyed a vogue in the mid-nineteenth century. The genre was still in full flower when the young Strindberg made his decisive mark as a dramatist of stature.

The prose version of *Master Olof* (1872) describes the young reformer's ordination on a Pentecost Saturday, in Strängnäs; his defiant pugnacity in his first clash with the Catholic bishops; and finally his appointment as preacher of the cathedral under King Gustav Vasa. It also recounts his private controversies with his pious and reactionary mother, his love-struggles with young Kristina, his intrigues against the King—whom he considers materialistic—and finally his plea for forgiveness on the penitents' bench.

The original conception for *Master Olof* was constructed with dramatic consistency. Olof, a young idealist filled with holy indignation, was to fight "spiritual death" on every front, and after his victory as reformer he was to continue his fight against the all-too-earthbound dictatorial King—but without success. Unbroken in spirit, he was to end on the scaffold.

Strindberg, however, hesitated to carry out this plan, because it was too greatly at variance with historical fact. True, the Master Olof of the prose version does, after long vacillation, ask for forgiveness, but the truly upright character in the play is Gert, who goes proudly to his death with the con-

Grace Kelly as LAURA, "that woman from hell,"
and Raymond Massey as the CAPTAIN in a New
York production of *The Father*, November 1949.
CULVER PICTURES, INC.

Scene from the 1971 Broadway production of *The Dance of Death*, starring Vivica Lindors as ALICE, Rip Torn as EDGAR, and Michael Strong as KURT.
ZODIAC

Opposite: Ingrid Thulin as the aristocratic and neurasthenic JULIE and Anders Ek as JEAN in a Stockholms Stadsteaters production of *Miss Julie*.
SWEDISH INFORMATION SERVICE

Anders Ek as CARL XII and Birgitta Valberg as
PRINCESS ULRIKA ELEONORA in a revival of
Carl XII at Stockholm's Royal Dramatic Theater.

Inga Tidblad as CHRISTINA is rebuked by her chancellor OXENSTIERNA in a scene from *Christina* at the Royal Dramatic Theater, Stockholm.

Tord Ståhl and Gunn Wållgren in a scene from a 1964 Stockholm production of Strindberg's first chamber play, *Thunderstorm*, at the Royal Dramatic Theater.

SWEDISH INFORMATION SERVICE

Opposite: Lena Nyman as BERTHA is shown in a scene from a 1968 Swedish production of *The Father*. Sif Ruud played the part of the old GOVERNESS.

SWEDISH INFORMATION SERVICE

In 1968 Sweden's Royal Dramatic Theater revived
The Pelican in its "second theater." Shown are Marie
Göranzon, Börje Ahlstedt, and Göran Graffman.
SWEDISH INFORMATION SERVICE

temptuous cry: "Apostate!" Strindberg himself was not wholly convinced by this ending, and after the play's initial rejection he proceeded to revise it.

Otherwise, the prose version is "a most remarkable work" of the twenty-three-year-old author: it ushered in a new era of Swedish drama. It presents us with altogether new rhythms and with much quicker time sequences than those then customary on the stage. One result was a much more rapid emotional impact: all the play's illogicalities and irrationalities become incidental. And those dramatic clashes—how they soar, utterly free of bourgeois deliberation or high-sounding lyricism, utterly free of pedantic idealistic tirades! Our young egocentric and nonconformist had simply written a drama about himself as the reformer. The work struck a blow for the freedom of spirit, a blow inspired by the necessity to think freely, to hold one's faith without coercion, and to be no man's servant. For in that summer of 1872, Strindberg's own freedom was threatened more severely than ever before.

Olof had left behind him the peaceful cloister at Strängnäs, to take up his militant lifework. Strindberg fled the bookish peace of his study in Uppsala, to throw himself into the uncertain battle for his creative vocation. Both Olof and Strindberg felt that they had been called; neither was willing to work merely for his daily bread. Olof declines a priestly office with disgust; Strindberg rejected the thought of entering his father's business, or becoming a civil servant.

When Strindberg realized that nobody wanted *Master Olof*, he suffered a series of crises. Late in 1874 and early in 1875, he radically revised the play. The result was the so-called interim drama, shorter by a third than the first version. In this new version, the course of the action is governed by remorseless laws of nature—it is no longer guided by the individuals' will. In the prose version, the play's realism has lost some of its bite, and the dialogue sounds instead a little declamatory and pompous. It is, all told, a colorless work.

But Strindberg did not give up. *Master Olof* had become an *idée fixe*. In May of 1875, he began to transform the play into a verse drama, and a year later it was finished. This version, too, is about one third shorter than the original. In theatrical terms, this version is more usable than the prose version, which must almost always be cut. Awkward rhyme and prose passages alternate and Strindberg used many single-line rejoinders, and set a rapid pace.

However, the new version lacked the hot breath of the prose drama. The fact that Olof actually accomplishes the reformation seems due less to his idealism and strong faith than to the success of Gert and the Catholics in raising his fighting spirit to that pitch of activity of which he is capable when seized by rage. After a partial success in the third act, Olof seems only mildly interested in Gert's subsequent machinations against the King.

In about 1877, Strindberg wrote an epilogue to the poetic version, a short piece with the notation "Fragment." In its introductory scene we meet our *pastor ordinarius* Olaus Petri a few years after the battles presented in the verse play. Utterly at peace now with the world and in the best of health, he had come into Stockholm through the North Gate, with his two sons, to watch a play.

That play is a comedy in six short scenes called

The Creation of the World and Its True Meaning.
Ironically, God represents the power of evil, and
Lucifer the lightbearer the power of good. God
creates the world and mankind for his own diver-
sion, while Lucifer, in the shape of a snake, brings
knowledge to Adam and Eve. God gives to man the
gift of love, but Lucifer wants to relieve man of the
misery of life by warfare, famine, and pestilence.
The Eternal One, enthroned high above the field of
battle, does not interfere. The comedy ends without
reconciliation, and the audience assaults the leading
actor because there is no happy ending.

The whole thing is a bitter entertainment, the
tired gesture of a young poet who had been stripped
of all illusions. Strindberg had found the material in
the fragment of a comedy *De Creatione Mundi*,
dating from the sixteenth century. With this gesture
ended six years of labor over a drama that no one
wanted to perform.

Anno 48
(*Anno fyrtioåtta*, 1876-77)

While continuing his vain attempts to
place *Master Olof*, in one version or another, with
one theater or another, Strindberg distracted himself by writing the now lost comedy *Gnat* (*Nag-
ging*, 1873), and the light play *Anno 48*, based on
the Stockholm uprisings in March of 1848.

The piece is a satire of a rich burgher, the brewer
Larsson, a splendidly crude royalist and reactionary,
who has surrounded himself with a court of more or

less eccentric protégés. Larsson is afraid of revolution, but makes his own modest contribution to bringing it about by proposing to the legislative assembly a law that would compel all servants to dress in gray, so that the military would know whom to shoot in case of disturbances.

The action flickers back and forth in brief scenes, the characters are illumined for only brief periods and then neglected. Nothing came of the work except a few short character sketches, which Strindberg later developed into full portraits in his novel *The Red Room.*

THE SECRET OF THE GUILD
(*Gillets hemlighet*, 1880)

While collecting material for his studies in cultural history, Strindberg had ample opportunity to acquaint himself with the activities of the medieval guilds. An historical event—a conflict among several architects as to which one of them would restore Uppsala Cathedral—gave him the idea for a play about the medieval builders' guild which had built the edifice.

Strindberg called *The Secret of the Guild* a "serious historical comedy." The action takes place in Uppsala, between the late fall of 1402 and the early spring of 1403. Its subject is the struggle between the stonecutter Sten and the mason Jacques over the question who will have the honor to continue work on the cathedral, which is still unfinished after 150 years of building. Jacques has little knowledge, and no original ideas; he is nervous, ambitious, desperate—and he drinks. He even swears a false oath claiming to know the secret of the guild: the ground plan of the cathedral. Sten, on the other hand, does have the necessary knowledge, he is talented, and "his heart is aflame with fervor"—not for the honor, but for the work itself.

The St. Lars Guild is in charge of the construction of the cathedral. When the guild's alderman, Jacques' father, had to retire because of age, Jacques is elected to succeed him. Elated, he demotes Sten from master to journeyman. Sten, in profound despair, wants to leave the country but is held back by his mistress and by the master of the cathedral. He humbly accepts his position, and obtains redress when the steeple erected by Jacques collapses in a storm. From that moment on, Jacques wallows in Schopenhauerian self-pity, and finds peace of mind because his wife stands by him.

The piece clearly represents the dramatic conclusion of a critical period in Strindberg's life, as does *To Damascus* later on. In both plays, arrogance is overcome, and reconciliation brought about, by sorrow. The author analyzes the causes of that sorrow. Already in this play, strange tormenting spirits appear and play their mysterious games, just as later happens in *To Damascus*. There are several sections where the dialogue is weaker than that in the prose version of *Master Olof*. In the years just past, Strindberg had worked more on epic than on dramatic material, and had only recently completed his great novel *The Red Room*. At times he is verbose, and archaisms hamper the flow of language.

LUCKY PER'S JOURNEY
(*Lycko-Pers resa*, 1882)

This fairy play, commissioned by the theater and stage director Ludvig Josephson, tells of the Swedish Peer Gynt who goes forth into the world to find his luck—but finds it only after he has ceased to want happiness for himself. The piece has strong touches of social satire, but also contains melancholy musings. Per, fifteen years old, has been locked up in a church steeple all his life. On Christmas Eve, he receives a magic wishing ring that makes all his dreams come true. He becomes a rich man, a famous reformer, a mighty Caliph, and a wayfarer in God's world of nature. But all his illusions are blown away. As the rich man, he has thousands of obligations and none but false friends; as the reformer, he is whipped in public, and sees through the sham of the world; as the Caliph, he is his own slave, his life is run by the will of the people. Nature is as cruel as it is beautiful. The one and only thing worth seeking is something Per cannot attain: love. Love comes to him only after his purification, as a gift of grace.

The piece is written at a lively pace, with short scenes reminiscent of film techniques. Magic and spoof follow each other in rapid succession; the dialogue flows easily as never before. For a satire, the play is uncommonly amiable and endearing; for a fairy tale, uncommonly free of sugariness. It carries no needless burden of philosophy; instead, it takes all the more delight in unmasking idealistic platitudes and peeping behind the glitter of false fronts. Moods shift and flicker, though some, such as Christmas Eve in the church steeple or the silent isolation of a village church, are well sustained.

SIR BENGT'S WIFE
(*Herr Bengts hustru*, 1882)

In his efforts to secure a good role for his first wife, Siri von Essen, Strindberg wrote *Sir Bengt's Wife*. For the first time in his dramatic career, he chose love and marriage as the central theme of his work. After four-and-a-half years of marriage, he had something to say on the subject.

Though Strindberg set the action in the sixteenth century, the historical mood fades as early as the second act and gives way to the portrayal of a "modern" marriage. Margit has been brought up in the romantic manner, and is disturbed when, on the morning after the wedding night, her knight picks his teeth. One irritation follows upon another. The lady's refined upbringing is in sharp contrast with the husband's plebeian manners, and when he threatens her with a beating she wants to divorce him. After numerous complications, during which she comes close to being seduced by a steward, and threatens to commit suicide, she is in the end reunited with Bengt.

Sir Bengt's Wife is a preliminary study for *Miss Julie*, but it is also—as Strindberg said himself—an expression of the struggle between the romantic and the realist within him; and finally, it is a gibe at Ibsen's Nora, who leaves the house, while Strindberg's Margit remains.

COMRADES
(*Kamraterna*, 1887)

Late in the summer of 1886, after he had left "that awful Grez . . . with those infernal modern ladies" and moved to Switzerland, Strindberg wrote the first act of his "first Swedish contemporary comedy." The four remaining acts were written toward the end of November, almost at one sitting. He called the piece *The Marauders* (*Marodören*, 1886), and offered it to Albert Bonnier, his publisher in Stockholm. But Bonnier refused to print it, and the important theaters in Scandinavia refused to perform it. On the advice of Hunderup, a theater director in Copenhagen, Strindberg finally agreed to make certain changes. He dropped the first act, retouched the others, and ended the play with the reconciliation of the marriage partners. He also changed the title to *Comrades*. However, he regretted the happy ending, and late in 1887 changed it to a brutal, somber conclusion.

The action takes place in the world of Parisian artists. The central figure is cigarette-smoking (1887!) Bertha, a painter with close-cropped hair and a masculine neckerchief. She refuses to sacrifice her art and to become the slave of any man; however, to improve her material circumstances she marries Axel, who is at first quite humble. When one of her paintings is accepted for an exhibition while Axel's work is rejected, she begins to humiliate her husband in every conceivable manner. At first he submits, but gradually he becomes more hostile; finally he throws her out of the house and acquires a mistress. He explains that the painting accepted for the exhibition was really his own, and that he had only switched numbers in order to let his wife have a success. Supporting the two main characters is a young lady named Abel, amusingly portrayed, with sympathies for women's liberation, bisexual tendencies, and a solid sense of reality.

The piece is written in a style betraying lively irritation. Strindberg strikes his blows against emancipated women living in companionate marriage—at first elegantly and with sadistic delight, but finally in a raging fury. Here, too, Strindberg turns against Ibsen's Nora: the wife so tyrannizes her cowed husband that she wants to force him to attend a masquerade costumed as a Spanish ballerina; finally he strikes back and subdues her. With this outcome, Strindberg has answered the prayers of his character Abel, who exclaims: "Alas, if I could only once, before I die, lay my eyes on such a marvelous freak: a man who dominates a woman!"

"The female vampire" (Bertha) here makes her first appearance in Strindberg's dramatic work. She has no inner life of her own—she merely drinks Axel's blood, like a parasite. Strindberg's favorite theme, the power struggle, comes off most convincingly when the clash of the contestants occurs in the sphere of a plausible conflict of ideas. But when, as in *Comrades*, he portrays a newly wed couple in which the husband is envious of every success of his beloved and hates her for it, while she in turn does everything to humiliate him, the audience may find it difficult to suppress a smile at their petty squabbles. However, if we do not take Strindberg's misogyny too seriously—and *Comrades* is presented ironically, as a comedy or even farce—the play can be quite effective.

THE FATHER
(*Fadren*, 1887)

In a letter to Edvard Brandes, Strindberg wrote that *Comrades* was meant to be the second part of a trilogy, whose first part would deal with "the father and Bertha's childhood." This first part, *The Father*, was written in the span of a few weeks. The first act was completed on February 6, and by February 15 Strindberg had finished the "tragedy in three acts."

Strindberg's marriage was then on the verge of collapse. He was overwrought, his imagination tended to run away with him, and at times he was not quite able to distinguish fantasy from reality. His general distrust assumed disquieting forms. Toward the end of the year 1886 his wife, concerned over his health and the family's future, had consulted a Swiss physician. Strindberg had learned of it, and leaped to the conclusion that she intended to have him locked away in an asylum and declared legally insane.

Strindberg had been reading books on hypnotism. In his new play, the man was to be portrayed as the weak partner, softened by civilization and doomed to be destroyed by a more primitive and more vigorous force—woman. The method of destruction was to be suicide induced by hypnotic suggestion. The victim was to be driven into compulsive fantasies, so that the cunning murder would look like the culmination of a tragic sickness. The tragedy was to be the drama of a love now dead—of a high-strung cavalry officer engaged in a merciless power struggle with his wife, of a man poisoned with the suspicion that he is not the father of his wife's child. In a blind fury, he eventually throws a lighted oil lamp into his wife's face. He is told that he is mentally unbalanced, and he is strapped into a straightjacket. He has a stroke and dies.

Clearly, Strindberg meant to show us how a woman can break even the strongest man. This is why he made his protagonist a military man, an officer. But military men are at times the easy dupes of intrigue. Strindberg's character, then, must also be highly educated, a leading scientist. A woman who could cut down such a giant would represent a mortal threat to the male sex.

When the piece was to have its Swedish première in 1908, at the Intimate Theater in Stockholm, Strindberg called Laura, the female lead, "that woman from hell." Indeed, it is difficult to discover the least trace of tenderness or kindness in this monster. The spectators see only her depravity, just as the officer himself sees her only through spectacles of hatred. She spreads her poison much like Iago—in Strindberg's own words, "the intrigue is no more insane than that of Iago murdering Othello's soul." Her actions are dictated by her lust for power. She gives a normal, motherly impression only during those few fleeting moments when her husband abandons the struggle and becomes gentle. In an astounding moment of self-knowledge, Laura eventually explains that she has not followed a preconceived plan, but has been compelled by a dark urge to remove her husband like an obstacle in her path. She is a demon, a nightmare, but at the same time a fanatic of the will, hysterical in the sense of the scientific knowledge of that time.

Her daughter Bertha, a volatile teen-ager, is torn back and forth between her parents, but succumbs to the stronger contestant—the woman. From *Comrades*, we know of Bertha's future fortunes as a marital failure and emancipated artist.

In no other play has Strindberg given as much individuality to his characters as in *The Father*. Even the minor roles are well-observed portrayals. The play's structure is firm throughout, maintaining the three unities: the action takes place within twenty-four hours, in one room, and remains focused on the question of paternity.

We must not disregard Strindberg's repeated assertion that the drama is to be taken as a creation of his imagination: "I feel as though I were walking in my sleep, as though fantasy and life were woven into one. I do not know whether *The Father* is a poetic fantasy or whether it is my life, but I sense that in the nearest future, at the given moment, it will become clear to me, and then I shall collapse —either in madness and with agonies of conscience, or through suicide. My ceaseless writing has turned my life into a shadow of life."

MISS JULIE
(*Fröken Julie*, 1889)

A young lady of noble birth, in a midsummer's night, allows herself to be seduced by her servant; next morning, out of repentance, she takes her own life. This is the whole simple action of the tragedy *Miss Julie*, Strindberg's most famous and most frequently performed drama. The final version of the piece is based on certain theoretical assumptions, developed by the author in a lengthy introduction which was to become as important for modern drama as the play itself. In it Strindberg formulated his principles of naturalistic drama, offering *Miss Julie* as an example.

According to Strindberg's prescription, the scenes must be as if they had been plucked from real life. Nothing must smack of "theater." He had avoided dividing the play into acts; real furniture was to take the place of painted stage property: there were to be no footlights; instead, the play was to be shown on a small stage in a small auditorium. None of the characters was to predominate, but their ensemble was to show a complex of various and divergent qualities. At the same time, and in keeping with Taine's theories, Strindberg drew his characters as though they were primarily determined by their heredity and environment. He avoided every trace of the contrived intrigue often to be found in Ibsen or mid-century French drama. Dialogue did not have to be absolutely logical in motivation—the characters were allowed to be moved by inexplicable impulse as readily as by calculation. To present reality without sham and without pastiche—that was his motto.

The action of *Miss Julie*, like that of *The Father*, is timebound. Since the spread of democracy, the social abyss separating servant and master has become much narrower than it was in the 1880s, and the distinction between nobles and commoners has become relatively insignificant. However, even in Strindberg's time it was considered unusual that a woman should kill herself because of an escapade.

The drama of *Miss Julie*, through many shrewdly

observed details, offers a rich description of the era
in which the piece was written. The dialogue is
masterful and reveals the characters as if they were
standing before us. There is Miss Julie, refined, extremely class conscious, but high-strung and uncon-
trolled because of her demanding but wholly
suppressed affections and drives, the pitiful product
of an undemocratic upbringing. There is Jean, pol-
ished in his own way, with the servant's habitual
deference but inwardly crude and ambitious, who
has been raised with a proletarian view of love.
Finally there is Kristin, solid, artless, soberly realistic, and endowed with a consciousness of her class
that is at least as pronounced as that of her mistress.

It is not easy, but all the more interesting, to trace
the origins of this finely articulated work. One of
its motivations must surely have been Strindberg's
own social inferiority complex. He suffered agonies
because of his lowly origins, especially when com-
paring himself with his wife, the baronness Siri von
Essen. To assert himself, he was only too happy to
embrace the theory that the future belonged to the
lower classes, while the nobility "with its deadly
prejudices about honor," was doomed to extinction.

However, a curious experience may well have
been the decisive influence that guided his choice
of plot. Although his marriage was already on the
brink of collapse in the summer of 1887, he and his
wife, in November of that year, went to Copenhagen together to see the première of *The Father*;
and in May of 1888 they moved into a kind of
pleasure mansion called Skovlyst (Forrest Joy),
near Copenhagen.

The mansion was presided over by the forty-year-
old Miss Louise Frankenau, who allowed herself to

be addressed as Countess. The house and its gardens were under the care of a steward named Ludvig Hansen, a suave and semi-elegant gypsy type with whom Strindberg at first got along very well indeed. Hansen was occupied with hypnotic experiments which he occasionally shared with Strindberg. From this material Strindberg fashioned the final scene, in which through hypnosis Jean influences Miss Julie to commit suicide.

Strindberg soon noticed that the steward dealt with his mistress on the most familiar terms, and assumed—as did the whole neighborhood—that he was the lover of "the Countess." Much later, it was revealed that Ludvig Hansen was Miss Frankenau's half-brother, but neither he, the illegitimate son, nor she, the legitimate daughter, ever wanted to reveal their relation, in deference to the memory of their father.

An icy chill prevaded the relation between Strindberg and his wife. They lived as celibates. During the summer, he took up with a housemaid at Skovlyst, the steward's seventeen-year-old daughter. Strindberg thought of himself as the aristocrat who had become involved with a lower-class woman for purely physical reasons. However, like Miss Julie, he experienced both the irresistible attraction of the bodies and the unbridgeable gulf separating the minds. We may wonder whether this interlude was not his strongest stimulus to write *Miss Julie*, though he himself speaks of a story in which a general's daughter seduces her stable boy.

Of all of Strindberg's dramas, *Miss Julie* is most thoroughly intellectualized in structure. As one surveys the long and varied fortunes of the play in different countries, the universal validity of

Strindberg's human portraits becomes clearer. Criticism that has been leveled at the play, apart from the claim that it was shocking, is concerned mostly with the final scene, in which Miss Julie commits suicide under hypnotic prompting. No doubt this suicide is dubious, like something taken from a book; even more so than are the madness and stroke of *The Father*.

In general, it may be said that Strindberg's interest in psychology and psychiatry had an enriching effect on his writings; it prompted him to return to belles-lettres. But like many other investigators of his day, Strindberg took such delight in new discoveries concerning the subconscious mind that he allowed himself to ascribe an all-too-wide validity to cases which were in fact exceptional.

In August 1888 Strindberg sent the piece to his Stockholm publisher, Bonnier, as "the first naturalistic tragedy in Swedish drama," with the note *ceci datera!* (It will go down in history!). The publisher declined it, and later called the rejection the greatest mistake of his entire career.

CREDITORS
(*Fordringsägare*, 1888)

This one-act play, written immediately after Miss Julie, presents a marital hell. Tekla, a novelist, has deeply offended her former husband Gustav by portraying him as an idiot in one of her novels. Gustav arrives to take revenge, and remains unrecognized by Tekla's present husband, the painter Adolf. In a diabolical conversation with

Adolf, who truly loves his wife and thinks the world of her, Gustav dissects Tekla's soul, and with his accusations reduces her to what she, in his view, really is: a polygamous nymphomaniac, a vampire who sucks men's spirits dry and then discards them as unwanted "creditors."

The dialogue is done with spiteful fury; it is barely mitigated by a touch of Schopenhauerian pity which, in the plays after *Inferno*, was to become a well-known catch phrase: "What a pity about men!" In form, the play is a further demonstration of Strindberg's thesis on modern naturalistic drama: "The action is as suspenseful," Strindberg wrote to his publisher, "as only the murder of a soul can be, analysis and motivations are exhaustive, the point of view is impartially deterministic, condemning no one, and at the same time explanatory and forgiving."

The Stronger
(*Den Starkara*, 1889)

While Strindberg was trying to track down a suspected infidelity on the part of his wife Siri, he himself was being besieged by a young Danish woman, Nathalia Larsen, who wanted to further her career by means of his plays. Siri, however, turned out to be the stronger woman—as she had on earlier occasions. The rivalry between the two actresses furnished Strindberg with the motif of this one-act play.

It deals with two actresses—Madame X, married, and Miss Y, single—who met in a café on the afternoon of Christmas Eve. Madame X does all the talking, Miss Y gives only mute responses. The play takes the shape of a "battle of minds," much like the one-act *Creditors*. There, two men fight over a woman; here, two women fight over a man.

The play is tailored to the needs of the Théatre Libre of Paris with its fifteen-minute plays. *The Stronger* is an outstanding achievement, an extremely astute study of female psychology.

PARIAH
(*Paria*, 1889)

Only a week later, on January 9, 1889, Strindberg finished another one-act play, *Pariah*. The piece deals once again with two anonymous "cases," the archaeologist X and the entomologist Y. Y has committed forgery but has not served sentence in his native country. Mr. X, who in his youth has killed a man but was never caught, is threatened with extortion by Mr. Y. However, with the logic of a master sleuth, Mr. X unmasks the forger and, thanks to his intelligence, emerges as the victor.

Originally *Pariah* had been meant to be merely a dramatization of a novel by Ola Hansson. Hansson, however, did not agree to Strindberg's proposal, feeling (rightly) that the novel was not really dramatic material. Strindberg, accordingly, worked out his own stage version, which contained little of the original. He changed the characters completely, and surrounded the test of strength between the two men with sharp highlights, drifting clouds, and

threatening storms. The play turns into a psychological "case study," a diagnosis in the manner of
that great master, Edgar Allan Poe.

HEMSÖ FOLK
(*Hemsöborna*, 1889)

Early in 1889 Strindberg was in worse
financial straits than usual. He had to repay a loan
to his brother Axel, and he needed funds for his
"Scandinavian Experimental Theater," as well as for
his own and his family's living expenses. He therefore resorted to a solution which he had tried to
avoid: he dramatized his novel *Hemsö Folk*. On
February 9, he informed his brother that the play
had been finished.

Except for his youthful *Hermione* (1870), it is
doubtful that Strindberg ever wrote anything as
unlike himself as this popular play. When he was in
the mood, Strindberg could create masterpieces with
a minimum of characters and scenes. But when his
imagination failed him, he tried to make up for
content by presenting a procession of numerous
characters with lively entrances and exits.

SIMOOM
(*Samum*, 1889)

At the end of February, 1889, Strindberg
wrote to his wife that he was engaged in writing
"Simoom, the desert wind of the Sahara, in which

you play an Arab girl who kills a French officer's soul." The piece—in which the desert wind "causes horrible visions that drive French soldiers to suicide"—was finished on March 4.

The action takes place in the second half of the nineteenth century, the period when the French with their Zouave regiments were attempting to consolidate their Algerian conquests. Biskra, a vengeful Arab girl, manages to hypnotize a French Lieutenant with the aid of the desert wind which "dries up the brains of white men like dates." The lieutenant believes that the sand is drinking water, horrible images pass before his feverish eyes, he dies. The drama is short, at bottom no more than a lengthy scene with strongly stylized dialogue.

THE KEYS OF THE KINGDOM OF HEAVEN
(*Himmelrikets nycklar*, 1892)

After an "emigration" of almost six years, Strindberg had returned to his homeland, worn-out, poor, and pursued by creditors. On top of it all, his marriage had entered its terminal crisis, and he greatly missed his children whom he loved tenderly —and who were still too small to hurt him. In the fall of 1891, while he was working on the first two acts of a new play, his children had been taken away from him. He had to seek a new kingdom of heaven. Christmas was imminent—a Christmas without children! Why not write a fairy tale for them, to be close to them at least through his writing?

But he could not quite get himself into a true

fairy-tale mood. The opening is grim—a heart-breaking scene in which the blacksmith mourns at the death bed of his three children. After Strindberg had given dramatic expression to the man's sorrow, his inspiration flagged. The result was something like a satirical fairy tale, with passages of fear-ridden seriousness, the testimonial of a searcher after God and of his life-and-death struggle.

The play's plot revolves around St. Peter's loss of the keys to the Kingdom of Heaven, and his decision to order a new set from the smith. The smith, however, cannot make new keys until he has seen the lock—the lock that is in heaven's gate. But where is heaven? A pitch-black pessimism marks the summing-up of a past which has just come to an end. There is only one thing that the smith does not want to give up, despite all reasons to the contrary—his search for heaven. For "when we have gone bankrupt here below, we yearn for what is up there, on high!"

THE FIRST WARNING
(*Första varningen*, 1892)

In March of 1892 Strindberg had once more turned to one-act plays, not least because the long five-acter, *The Keys of the Kingdom of Heaven*, had found no theater willing to take it. Between March and September, he wrote six one-act plays. The first of these was probably *The First Tooth* (*Första tanden*, 1892), later renamed *The First*

Warning, a comedy of jealousy written in the stylish French manner.

The play provides an insight into the relation of absolute passion between husband and wife. The man has often wished that his wife was disfigured with pockmarks so that he might overcome his relentless jealous doubts. The wife, in turn, has had to realize that his love for her flags whenever he has no cause for jealousy. The couple have no children. She is a singer—and her admirers send her flowers. He is jealous; he has already deserted her six times, and is about to leave her for the seventh time. At this point, luckily, she breaks a front tooth; she interprets this as a sign of approaching old age. By a coincidence, she also surprises her husband in a compromising situation with a baroness and her daughter. Now it is her turn to be jealous—which in turn inclines her husband to be forgiving—and all ends well as the two, both reassured, go traveling together.

DEBIT AND CREDIT
(*Debet och kredit*, 1892)

This one-act play derived from Strindberg's personal circumstances. He had had to take his clothes to the pawnbroker, and could barely afford to buy firewood. No wonder that he wrote of his misery, chosing as his hero a man in high position who is without money and hunted by creditors.

On his return from Africa, Axel, an explorer, is

showered with honors and with the claims of his old creditors. When a whole company of creditors of every sort invades his home, he simply leaves the room.

Strindberg himself, in tight situations, had used this same strategy. As a study of an intelligent man's pitiful behavior, the play is without finesse, though the author stressed his hero's intelligence and tried to overlook his cowardice. The whole thing seems like a variation on the "battle of the brains."

FACING DEATH
(*Inför döden*, 1892)

During his divorce proceedings, Strindberg often toyed with the thought of suicide. His solitude, and the sad return to a bachelor's life, were torture to him; besides, he was afraid that Siri might speak ill of him to their children. His one-act play *Facing Death*, completed as "a tragedy in nine scenes," is the author's self-defense.

The action takes place in a Swiss pension on the brink of financial collapse. The owner, Monsieur Durand, is tired and overworked, and choses a desperate way out to escape from ruin: to secure his fire and life insurances for his three daughters, he sets the house afire and kills himself in the flames.

Strindberg apparently expected that the public would feel profound pity for Durand. However, what we see is a family with abnormally strong emotions, a hysterical man, and inadequate daughters. We are sorry for all of them, but cannot pity them because how they came to be what they are remains obscure.

MOTHERLOVE
(*Moderskärlek*, 1892)

With this play Strindberg once again attacks a mother, and defends the self-sacrificing and maligned father. But this time the tone of his attack upon the mother is considerably sharper. She is described as a forty-two-year-old "former prostitute," and her friend, a wardrobe keeper, as a procuress.

The scene is a bathing resort on one of Stockholm's islands, where the mother is staying with her twenty-year-old daughter and the wardrobe keeper. To prevent her own past from being revealed, the mother maligns the girl's father and uses every means to prevent contact between father and daughter; in fact, she cuts the girl off from the outside world. But her strategy fails. The daughter learns what a noble and unselfish man her father actually is, and what a compromising past her mother has. But her bond with the two women has meanwhile grown so strong that the girl can no longer cut herself loose.

Outside, in the radiant sunshine on the islands, whiteclad youngsters sail and play tennis—while in the house a worn-out whore and her slatternly friend drink, smoke, and slam cards on the table, converse in bitter, vulgar language, curse the upper classes, spout sentimentalities, and keep a young girl under lock and key. This selfish mother is evidence of Strindberg's private injury.

Playing with Fire
(*Leka med elden*, 1892)

Siri von Essen had meanwhile gone to Finland with the three children. In midsummer of 1892 Strindberg, lonesome and forlorn, composed this one-acter quivering with eroticism.

The action of this play also takes place on a warm summer's day on one of the islands. A group of five people in comfortable circumstances—a young painter and his wife, his parents, and a cousin—are trying to while away the time. Sweet idleness and monotony render them highly susceptible. They are joined by Axel, a young man about to be divorced. He and the painter's wife need not play with fire very long before her passion bursts into open flame. The painter gives his wife her freedom, but demands that Axel marry her. Axel, however, is disenchanted by his first marriage, and hurriedly leaves the house.

The whole action takes place in the morning, before breakfast. The play ends as the original group of five sit down together with fresh appetites to eat fried flounders.

Few of Strindberg's plays are as striking as is this one in what is said between the lines. It is no surprise that the play proved to be his most successful one-acter. Young Axel is in many ways Strindberg's alter ego, portrayed with a pleasing touch of self-irony. "But it is a difficult piece," Strindberg wrote, "because it is meant tragically, yet has a semi-comical ending."

THE LINK
(*Bandet*, 1892)

Despite his preference for comedy, Strindberg's imagination returned again and again to his marriage, which was approaching complete collapse. In the last one-act play he wrote that summer, he finally turned to the divorce proceedings themselves.

The action takes place in a court of law. When the protagonists, a baron and his wife, entered marriage, they had been very foresighted—just as Strindberg and his wife had been—and made a written agreement that neither would make proprietary claims upon the other. But the baron had tired of introducing as his wife the woman who was now his friend's mistress, and now the two are standing before the judge, firmly resolved to maintain their dignity and not let their private lives be besmirched before the scandal-hungry public. The judge raises the question of whether the baroness shall have the right to raise the son—"memento of our hours of beauty, the link that ties our souls together"—and angry mutual accusations erupt. In the end, neither partner is given custody of the child. Faced with this catastrophe, however, the two experience a feeling of something like community, and the baron comes to realize that it is not God but nature "which incites us to mutual hatred, and to mutual love."

Without this final scene, the vigorous drama would have remained merely a naturalistically constructed report on court proceedings. As it is, it turns into a true drama about the nature of love, though the principal male role lacks psychological depth.

To Damascus, Part I
(*Till Damaskus I*, 1898)

Nearly six years were to go by before Strindberg began his next play, a drama which he would eventually develop into a trilogy. The first part of *To Damascus* was finished in March 1898, in Paris; the second on July 17 of the same year, in Lund. The third was not completed until the summer of 1901, in Stockholm.

To Damascus traces the outlines of that development which critics like to call "Strindberg's conversion." He had definitely overcome his short atheistic period, and resumed his former stance toward God. His reorientation was mainly the result of his experiences during the so-called *Inferno*-crisis in Paris. From December 1896 onward, Strindberg was once again in Sweden; initially he settled in Lund.

His readings in the works of Emanuel Swedenborg had convinced Strindberg that, strictly speaking, he had been in hell. Like Dante, he had walked through an Inferno. He had been pursued by none other than a just but merciful God who meant to purify him. Punishment and suffering were a grace of God. With every new suffering, Strindberg imagined, the Lord had canceled out a debit entry in his account book. The instrument which the All

Mighty employed to drive all sinners to repentance and reconciliation Strindberg called "the powers." The supreme task of the powers, Strindberg thought, was to destroy his own arrogance, his hubris, which he felt to be a mortal sin. But Strindberg's new attitude by no means signified that he acknowledged orthodox Christianity. His animosity toward Christ remained unchanged. He meant to settle his accounts with God directly, without the aid of any mediator, because he considered it demeaning to owe a debt of gratitude to anyone.

In *To Damascus I*, Strindberg describes how The Unknown, a poet who feels that he is hounded by misfortune, comes to realize that his fate is actually guided by a kind Providence. He must undergo numerous humiliations; he cuts a miserable figure before the lady with whom he has fallen in love and eloped. Being without means, he becomes painfully dependent on her relatives, and in the end abandons everything. He falls down a steep mountain slope and, grievously injured, is brought to a strange cloister asylum. All the while he is tormented by a vague fear, the feeling that someone is pursuing him and directing his fate. The Unknown's conscience is aroused when his father-confessor reads to him the curses in the Books of Moses against those who do not obey the voice of the Lord. He feels that he has led the life of a scoundrel, and has an intimation that God has sent him suffering in order to cleanse him. This insight comes to him through a series of fortuitous events. He makes his fortune, and is reunited with his lady. But he still has his doubts at the door of the church into which the lady wishes to entice him: "I'll be glad to go through it, but I won't stay!"

Strindberg here was drawing on personal experiences. The autobiographical components of the play, in themselves artistically indifferent, have been selected and tied together with extraordinary skill. At the play's beginning, The Unknown is not an atheist. He had been an atheist earlier, but now he has gained understanding. The author depicts how The Unknown, in an agonizing struggle with the Invisible, is forced to change his views, and to accept the existence of a just Providence that metes out punishment proportionate to the sins committed.

The Unknown, in his struggle with God, has to pass certain stations along his road of suffering, similar to Christ on the road to Golgotha. The sequence of these stations was of considerable importance to Strindberg in structuring the drama. We find an intimation of his technique as early as *Lucky Per's Journey*; there, as now in the *Damascus* play, the church is both the protagonist's point of departure and his goal. Strindberg described the first part of *To Damascus* as "a new genre, fantastical and luminous like *Lucky Per*, but taking place in the present, and in full reality."

The wander-drama, presented as a fairy tale with only occasional dream passages, has here become a wander-drama whose structure approaches that of the dream plays. It has been transposed to a subtler psychic atmosphere where wondrously amazing encounters and disappearances, magic and unreality, are arranged to reflect complex psychic experiences: a drama of a journey in the landscape of the soul.

One of the pioneering achievements of this play is the consummate ease with which Strindberg made the exponents of the subconscious mind—the beggar, Caesar, the patients in the asylum—enter into fullest reality, without indicating whether they were dream images or figments of the imagination. Numerous passages consist of visions, and of experiences of which he himself, during the period of his worst crisis, could not tell with certainty whether they reflected reality or existed only in his imagination. By transforming the subconscious into characters who take part in the action, Strindberg made it possible to write an ego-drama. The Invisible (God), however, is not a representation of the ego. He appears only indirectly; his function as the counterpole of The Unknown is performed by other visible characters—the mother, the prostitute, the physician, and so on. In this way, *To Damascus I* became a model for that type of expressionistic drama which portrays reality and its shapes, not as an objective observer sees them, but as they appear to the subject whose sovereign imagination enlarges or suppresses reality's shapes at will.

In the rather conventional history of the literature of the stage, *To Damascus* is the first play to bear witness that the subconscious plays a primary role in the interpretation of the human psyche. A straight line of development runs from Strindberg's drama to Kafka and O'Neill, and on to the theater of the absurd of Ionesco, Adamov, and Vian.

To Damascus, Part II
(*Till Damaskus II*, 1898)

Three circumstances, it seems, prompted Strindberg to continue the *Damascus* drama. One was the final reckoning with the "lady," connected

with his separation from Frida Uhl, his second wife;
next, there was the utter failure of his pseudo-
scientific attempts to make gold; and finally, he
was in dread of the possibility that his children,
then in Finland, might have a stepfather.

To Damascus II is so filled with autobiographical
details that the author now and again allows himself
to be distracted from the true dramatic line. An
example is the struggle between The Unknown and
God, who is personified by the "spirit of discipline,"
the father confessor, who is also identified as a
Dominican monk and a beggar. In *Part II* the pace
has slackened, but on the other hand, the muted
means of expression have been sharpened. The light
is colder, the marital debates are more heated, the
supernatural is more calculated. The guilt complexes
seem exceedingly involved and improbable. The
lady is initially married to the Confessor; she then
becomes the mistress of a married painter; next, she
compels the physician to marry her, only to desert
him and marry The Unknown a second time.

Certain scenes stand out with truly magic power
—the alchemist's banquet, for example. The slovenly
tavern is in sharp contrast with its somber background, as in a Rembrandt painting, but it is also
visionary, macabre, full of noise and melancholy—
Dostoevskian. One feels that one is truly face to face
with the still unequaled first beginning of stage
expressionism. The stage directions for the transi-
tion from the scene in the tavern to that in prison—
when The Unknown is catapulted from supreme
triumph into deepest disgrace—are indicative:

> Darkness. A jumble of stage decorations—
> landscape, palace, living room—are lowered

from above and shoved in from the wings so that furniture and persons disappear—last of all The Unknown who stands like one paralyzed, asleep. Finally he, too, is covered from view. Out of the jumble, a prison cell emerges.

The scenes in the tavern are intended to give a picture of the soul's struggle rather than of reality, and the events on stage are intended to make this struggle visible to the audience. The extent to which this is true can be gathered from the grim humor at The Unknown's exit; like a stage director, the physician calls to the slovenly tavern crowd: "Infernal howls of the victims!" This is promptly confirmed by Strindberg's own stage directions, which read: "The guests howl."

ADVENT
(*Advent*, 1898)

With the play *Advent*, aptly described by the author as a "fairy-tale tragedy," Strindberg passed from introspection to a look at the outside world. His critical eye alighted upon two people— Frida Uhl's comfortable grandparents. As so often before, an increasingly aggressive mood seized Strindberg the more he thought about people with whom he had been in conflict. His fury had obviously reached just the right pitch when he wrote *Mausoleum* (*Mausolén*), later called *Advent*.

The play is a fairy tale about the just punishment of an unjust judge and his evil wife, told as a story for grown-up children. The form changes from that of a fairy story to that of an *Inferno* dream, becoming a mystery pastiche with realistic insertions. The piece opens quite peacefully, as the old judge and his wife converse about the mausoleum which they have had built for themselves as a dignified last resting place. But the conversation becomes more and more Pharisaic. They praise their own good fortune, well deserved they believe, and look down with contempt on all who have fared less well. The vengeance of the "powers" is not long in coming—a veritable witches' sabbath of fearful visions. In the dark of night, a procession of strange figures passes by, including Death with his scythe and a decapitated sailor carrying his head in his hand. Are they ghostly shades, or feverish dreams? The devil, appearing in the shape of a penniless schoolmaster, used his cane on the self-satisfied old judge. The judge's wife is lured to attend a ghostly ball, where gloomy musicians with chalk-white faces play and the guests dance slowly in funereal rhythms. The judge is brought into a courtroom, bells ring, chairs move about, an ax on the wall stirs, the sentence is announced—though not a single human presence becomes visible. In the fifth act, the judge's wife freezes to death in a morass while the judge is stoned to death by those he has unjustly condemned. The two meet again in the valley of hell. When they are at last purified and come to understand their guilt, the advent star, the star of hope, lights up on the horizon.

The piece is overly rich in fantasy, but the author's *Inferno* ideas provide a thread that can be traced through all the strange tissue of macabre visions and fairy stories. Here, as in earlier pieces, Strindberg is pondering once more the problem

which pursued him always: the meaning of suffering. The severe punishment suffered by the judge
and his wife is easily understood in the light of their
evil deeds—but that innocents, too, are afflicted is
not so easy to understand. The poet finds this
answer: "Those who are guilty and condemned
suffer justly, and their suffering does them no honor:
but to suffer unjustly is a divine grace and trial, and
yields a golden harvest to those who remain stead-
fast."

THERE ARE CRIMES AND CRIMES
(*Brott och brott*, 1899)

The crimes of the judge and his wife in
Advent were crude and obvious crimes; but in the
piece Strindberg wrote immediately afterward, the
crime was one that he himself had committed, and
it was vastly more subtle. The new play, written in
January and February 1899 in Lund, indicated the
difference by its title, *There Are Crimes and Crimes*.

It seems plausible that Strindberg, in the course
of the divorce proceedings that were to separate
him from Frida Uhl, actually wished that his daughter Kerstin had never lived—the daughter whose
affection he had purposely shunned. In thought, he
had committed a crime—he had become the murderer of his own child. He jotted down the basic
motif of the new drama: "The evil will brings on
punishment, just like an evil deed. . . . He curses the
life of his child, the child dies, he is suspected and
accused." Some years earlier, according to *Inferno*,
he had performed manipulations with his daughter's

portrait. He imagined himself capable of inducing mild illness in his child by way of magic (occult experiments at a distance were in fashion at the time), so that he would have an excuse to go to Austria and to see Kerstin—and her mother—again.

The play tells how the dramatist Maurice has an enormous success on the Parisian stage, and falls head over heels in love with the sculptress Henriette. He takes the place of her current lover Adolphe, and totally forgets his own faithful Jeanne, by whom he has had a child. On the morning after the première, he wishes for his daughter's death so that he may devote himself wholly to Henriette. Punishment promptly follows: the child dies. Maurice, tormented by pangs of conscience, is suspected of murder. His play closes, his relation with Henriette cools, his friends desert him. However, an investigation determines that the child has died of natural causes. Maurice regains the respect of the world, and his work is again performed. In a church, he talks to his God to rid himself of the guilt of his thought. He has ended his relations with both Jeanne and Henriette. Like The Unknown in *To Damascus, Part II*, he has learned to see the worthlessness of the lures of the world: "Honor is an illusion, gold is chaff, women are like intoxicating liquor!"

Though Strindberg attacks the evil will, the secret crime, he defends it at the same time with characteristic ambivalence. He makes Adolphe claim that "no one is truly a good man who has not committed a crime," and that the average human being "who never says an evil word and forgives everything" is in all likelihood someone who must atone for a secret trespass. The result of this line of thought is, obviously, that a crime is something good, indeed, that it is a grace bestowed from on high, provided it is followed by pangs of conscience and purification through suffering.

THE FOLKUNG SAGA
(*Folkungasagan*, 1899)

Strindberg had suffered, he had been purified, and he had come to understand the causes. At first in violent opposition to his God, he had now understood his guilt and become a penitent on the road to reconciliation.

He found an early parallel to his own fate in Sweden's turbulent history during the fourteenth century, at the time of King Magnus Eriksson. In early April of 1899 he resumed work in Lund. *Magnus the Good*, as the five-act drama was originally called, was finished on April 20.

The action begins with a parade in honor of Magnus' birthday. His good fortune is unmarred. Skåne has become Swedish, Carelia has been freed from the Russians, the serfs have been liberated, the peasants are protected by law. He is being celebrated as a prince of peace and liberator—but his hubris is punished by the envious gods. The Russians have won a victory over the Swedes near Göteborg, but Magnus nonetheless gives thanks to his God for still having his wife, his son, and his loyal friends. At this moment, the Possessed One appears on a balcony and prophesies that the King's wife will deceive him with his friend, that the King's murderer will have carnal knowledge of the King's widow, that the King's son is planning to overthrow his father, that a bishop will banish him, and that the southern Swedes will revolt. He moreover prophesies that plague will sweep the country— and all this because the crown of Magnus, himself guiltless, is stained with blood.

The action has many ramifications, branching out from a cluster of religious and ethical problems. The author frequently elaborates on the question how the Lord will score the symphony He is about to perform. The ancient Greek conceptions of nemesis and hubris are interwoven with ideas from the Old and New Testaments. Strindberg captures the medieval mood in striking mass scenes with very effective contrasts. Crudeness is contrasted with the mysticism of suffering, supernatural lyricism with sadistic brutality. Boundless sloth burgeons in the wake of the plague. Fear-ridden, faceless multitudes cower in the shadows.

In the dialogues between Ingeborg, the royal widow, and Duke Knut Porse the hate-love of the earlier dramas is expressed at white heat—an intimation of the later drama *The Dance of Death*.

Gustav Vasa
(1899)

Gustav Vasa, founder of the Swedish realm, was the central figure of Strindberg's next play, completed in mid-June of 1899.

Only rarely in his dramatic work did Strindberg portray his characters with as much objectivity as in this work. In Sweden it is considered his most popular and his most artistically accomplished play. It is Swedish to the core, but without any patriotic pathos. The weakness of historical plays, of course, is usually that we know beforehand how they will end. Rare indeed are the pieces that can keep the outcome a secret with as much cunning and for as long as *Gustav Vasa*. Structurally the play is a true masterpiece. Strindberg, with astute calculation, built up extraordinary dramatic tension around his protagonist by not bringing Gustav Vasa on stage until the third act. The first act, a work of genius in its effectiveness, has so much inner unity that it could almost be performed as an independent one-act play. Here Strindberg meant to present, in the form of a drama from Swedish history, the selfsame religious and moral experiences he had presented in the visions of the *Damascus* drama: that only that man will partake in the splendor of divine grace who bows in humility and accepts his punishment in the realization that it is just and has been imposed by kind Providence.

ERIK XIV
(1899)

The opening scene of Strindberg's next historical play, *Erik XIV*, takes place on the same castle terrace as *Gustav Vasa*'s closing scene. Karin, the king's mistress, is conversing with the love of her youth, young ensign Max, when suddenly a hail of nails, pillows, shoes, and other objects descends upon them from a balcony. Up on the balcony stands King Erik, distrustful and displeased.

The King's mood does not improve as he now learns from Nils Sture that Elizabeth of England has scorned his request for her hand in marriage. The King decides to take revenge upon Sture's klan for this insult, because he imagines that they rejoice at his failure, and because they are loyal to his brother. However, the accusations he presents to the Estates in Uppsala are so confused that the Sture klan is cleared; the King thereupon orders them stabbed to death in their prison cells. In the final act, he legalizes his relation with Karin, and invites a crowd of riffraff to a marriage feast. But the dukes Carl and Johann also come to the wedding, and they take the King prisoner.

King Erik and Göran Persson are among the most interesting roles ever created on the Swedish stage. Strindberg's Erik, "the characterization of a man without character," is impulsive, moody, spoiled, thoughtless, and pleasure-mad. He is most at ease in the company of simple folk, because he deems himself their intellectual superior, and because he inclines to the more primitive appetites. He is a psychopath, insanely distrustful and choleric. And Göran Persson? He is by no means merely the colorless boon-companion of a half-mad king, but is portrayed as a subtle, active politician and a shrewd lawyer. With this characterization, Strindberg anticipated the results of later research, which showed Göran Persson to have been a learned man and clever jurisprudent, ruthless in the Machiavellian spirit of the Renaissance.

GUSTAV ADOLF
(1900)

For no other historical play did Strindberg prepare himself as thoroughly as for his *Gustav Adolf*. Even though he had previously stated publicly that he intentionally altered historical events for dramatic effect, he now clearly wanted to refute the repeated criticism that he distorted history in his plays.

In a vast drama of an historical journey, we follow Gustav Adolf on his far-flung campaigns in Germany—from his landing at Usedom, through wartorn lands swarming with beggars and marauders, across the battlefields near Leipzig, through the gorges of Thuringia, past a pleasure castle near Mainz and army camps reeking with death, into a mist-shrouded smithy near Lützen, and finally to the castle church of Wittenberg, where the King lies on his deathbed.

It is a formless drama, the longest one-part drama that Strindberg ever wrote. Numerous minor characters are introduced, historical recapitulations and genealogical sequences crowd the pages; the dramatic drive often falters, and the lack of a central conflict has troublesome consequences.

Despite all this, the play has a number of intensely searing scenes that by far transcend all lifeless scholarship; indeed, they assume a dramatic life of their own. The play's thesis is syncretistic: the forms of religion may change, but God is One. It is pointless to fight over religious differences. However, the closer Gustav Adolf comes to this insight, the less clear-cut becomes his purpose; this fact makes the dramatic composition difficult.

Midsummer
(*Midsommar*, 1900)

Strindberg had at last established himself as Sweden's leading dramatist. Starting in the eighties, he had regained his position as Sweden's most-talked-about author. Even the mails now brought him requests for his work. Stage director Albert Ranft asked him to write a new play, to be performed at the reopening of the rebuilt South Theater (Södra Teatern) in Stockholm. (In the event, matters did not work out that way.)

The work, which Strindberg finished on July 26, 1900, was called *Midsummer Journey* (*Midsommar-resan*) but in the proof stage was renamed *Midsummer*, "a serious comedy in six acts." It was a broad portrayal of an era, rather than a stage drama. In *Midsummer*, the author described the astonishing changes he had noted in Swedish society on his return from his difficult years abroad. "Wine, women, and song and all that. . . . We have exchanged them for a little seriousness, for duty and work, a healthy body, a house of our own, for sick care, old age security, and child care."

Strindberg had intended to write a cozy, heart-warming popular play—but whenever he turned to cozy, heartwarming subjects he slipped immediately into overly detailed descriptions of social settings, and introduced a swarm of roles without sharp char-

acterization. Nor did he want to dig into their characters, for he did not believe that there was such a
thing as men who are good and warm-hearted to
the core.

CASPER'S SHROVE TUESDAY
(*Kaspers fet-tisdag*, 1900)

Midsummer included a Punch-and-Judy
show. For his own entertainment, Strindberg now
sat down to write another such show, a carnival
piece without satire or deeper significances, but
rather a pastiche with an extremely simple plot line.

A Punch-and-Judy showman and his wife arrive
at a cemetery in Stockholm. They have just re-
deemed their large chest of puppets from the pawnbroker and are about to dress their little performers
for the spring opening in the zoo. While the director
goes to get paint, the puppets leap from the box
and disport themselves. Death insists on a higher
salary than all the others.

EASTER
(*Påsk*, 1900)

Strindberg's alter ego here is the schoolmaster Elis, melancholy and defiant like the author
himself. The central figure of the play, however, is
the "Easter maiden" Eleonora. Strindberg's deep
compassion for his sister Elizabeth, a pathological
melancholic who was later to die in Uppsala, prob-

ably provided an important stimulus for this passion drama. Strindberg felt closer to Elizabeth than to his other siblings; he believed that her fate and his own were linked by a mystic tie.

The action looks like a family tragedy. The father is in prison for embezzlement, while the mother remains firmly convinced that his innocence will someday be established. Elis, the son, has to provide for the whole family, which includes his mother, his bride Kristina, his mentally ill sister Eleonora, and their roomer, Benjamin, whose money the father has embezzled. The father's misdeed has driven the family into isolation. A mood of gloom pervades the household. They all live in the constant fear that their creditor Lindkvist will seize their furniture. Benjamin is depressed because he has failed his Latin examination, Elis is disgruntled because his bride wants to go to a concert with his rival. Eleonora is afraid of the police, because she has picked up a narcissus plant (the Easter flower) in a flower shop, and now fears that the florist may not have found the money she left for him.

The final act begins under a cloudy sky, and ends in bright spring sunshine. Lindkvist, the creditor, proves merciful, because Elis' father had once shown him understanding in a difficult situation. Eleonora's "crime" is cleared up. Elis and Kristina make up. At the end of their road of suffering, the family has come to understand that it is not only evil deeds that return to haunt the culprit—good deeds, too, return.

Strindberg's success in creating so much suspense around Good Friday, a day when next to nothing happens in a small town, is truly astounding. He is a master of the art of rendering a state of fear through the imaginative magnification of realistic details, especially in the final scene, a splendidly realized confrontation between the generous creditor Lindkvist and the cocky young Elis. The inner life of all the characters seems large and spacious, precisely because it is set in the tight confines of a small town. The family lives as if embattled in a fortress, isolated by its own distrust, concerned with its prestige to the point of aggressiveness.

The piece deals with the aftereffects of a crime, a Dostoevskian theme. This parallel is underlined by the mystical allusions to Christ's passion, focused especially in the role of Eleonora. Eleonora is a poetic figure of light who leads a life burdened with bitterness. In Strindberg's view, she represents suffering—she atones for the guilt of mankind. Her character is good beyond measure because she has been cleansed and purified beyond measure. Here as in *Advent*, Strindberg fuses the Schopenhauerian theme of suffering with the Christian faith in deliverance. Elis, who again and again stresses the Old Testament idea "not mercy, only justice," is finally forced to his knees. The torment of the present is fanned by the winds of the gospel of forgiveness— a revelation which in Strindberg's world comes almost always as a surprise.

Easter, more even than *Advent*, is a modern mystery play. But it is at the same time a morality play, whose occasionally trite theses must be balanced by the irrationalism and complexities of the characters.

The Dance of Death
(*Dödsdansen*, 1900)

After taking up his final residence in Stockholm in the fall of 1899, Strindberg lived a very retiring life, devoting himself ardently to his studies and writing. Early in October, he began work on *The Dance of Death*, the portrayal of a marital hell; he finished it a year later.

The artillery captain Edgar and his wife Alice are about to celebrate their silver wedding anniversary. No doubt there will be speeches eulogizing their faithful union through twenty-five years of marriage; surely a toast will be drunk to them. However, these expectations seem a cruel joke, because the two live in an ancient castle-tower on an island. The servants will not stay because they have been treated discourteously, and nobody else wants to have dealings with them since they have withdrawn into their world of malice. They spend their lives without any higher interests, in corrosive monotony.

A change occurs only with the arrival of Kurt, who has been transferred to the island as a quarantine officer. Both partners seek to please him. In the end, a crisis arises when the captain, during a grotesque dance, sinks to the floor unconscious. Alice believes him dead and rejoices at her liberation. But she rejoices too soon. Edgar recovers, and out of vengefulness pretends that he has started divorce proceedings, whereupon she denounces him for embezzlement. But neither event alters the situation, life goes on as before; again, the partners are making plans for their wedding anniversary.

Why did it have to come to this? Because in Strindberg's typical stage marriages both partners insist explicitly upon their right. They are self-centered and, passionate as they are, cannot control their tempers. They are capable of turning the fleeting moment into a festive occasion, but in the monotony of daily life together they fall victim to their own moodiness. The similarity between this and other marriages described by Strindberg is striking. Memories play their part—for example, Strindberg's own memory of his confrontation with the Captain of the Guard Carl Gustaf Wrangel and the dramatist's wife Siri, who complained that marriage had ruined her artistic career.

We must stress here in all justice that Strindberg —after thoroughly exposing Edgar and Alice and their common malice—looks at human fate with Schopenhauerian compassion, and with the equally Schopenhauerian hope that life may turn out to be a bad dream which is long since past. *The Dance of Death*, however, is not merely honest realism in a symbolic framework; it is also the product of an early dream-play period.

The first part of *The Dance of Death* takes place in autumn. The second part, however, probably added on by Strindberg in December of 1900, takes place in a drawing room bright with the summer sun. The island is bathed in sunlight, young people are playing games and carrying on flirtations.

The exposure of Edgar occurs at a furious pace. He exploits Kurt, steals his ideas, ousts him from his position, and seizes his property. Yet all his machinations are frustrated, surprisingly, by the death of their daughter Judith: the captain has a stroke, and dies. Strindberg gives a fiery and intense description of Judith's love for Allen, Kurt's shy son. There is a fascinating brief and passionate encounter between the two, lashed by wind and rain, heated and reckless. Suffering carries the day even with people in their tender youth when they are struck by love. The dance goes on.

THE BRIDAL CROWN
(*Kronbruden*, 1901)

Around the turn of the century, folklore and patriotism were very popular in Sweden. These enthusiasms drew their sustenance especially from Dalarna, where Gustav Vasa, founder of the realm, once fought it out with the unruly Dala peasants. Strindberg was steeping himself then in the sagas from Dalarna. During his studies, *The Bridal Crown* took shape in his mind, and on January 5, 1901 the piece was completed.

Kersti, a young Daleswoman, has given birth in secret to a son by her lover Mats, and smothers the child in order to make a marriage as an honest bride. Tormented by ghostly apparitions, the emanations of her guilty conscience, she confesses her crime on the wedding day. Crushed with remorse and disgrace, she meets Christ in the guise of a child, and finds peace—but an ancient feud between her family and Mats' flares up anew. The feud is settled only after Kersti, on Easter morning, walking from prison to the church to do her penance, breaks through the ice and drowns.

The Bridal Crown is a mixture of ghost-play and Dala saga, a dramatic poem on the theme of crime, punishment, and atonement. The violent action is accompanied by the Water Sprite's sad and lonely song. Strindberg himself composed the melody—his only known complete musical composition—a melancholy, monotonous air he used to hum to himself as he sat alone in a corner of the Bohemian tavern "At the Black Suckling" in Berlin.

A powerful stimulus for *The Bridal Crown* came from Strindberg's concern for his daughter Greta, and his desire to write an attractive role for her when she was planning to become an actress. Her Nordic type and Finnish-accented Swedish seemed to him good qualifications for the role of Kersti—which Greta Strindberg was in fact to play many times.

Swanwhite
(*Svanevit*, 1901)

Early in 1901 began Strindberg's stormy love affair with the twenty-two-year old Norwegian actress Harriet Bosse. The first literary fruit of their friendship was *Part III* of *To Damascus*; the second was *Swanwhite*, which he gave to Harriet Bosse as a bridal gift when they became engaged on March 5, 1901.

The form of the play shows the influence of an early work by Maurice Maeterlinck, the fairy play *Princess Maleine* (*La Princesse Maleine*, 1889), which Strindberg, according to his diary, had read a month earlier. The play tells how an evil step-mother separates a prince and a princess, in order that the prince may marry her own daughter. In his novel *Vivisections* (1894), Strindberg had emphasized that he had high regard for the childlike naïve charm of the early Maeterlinck, but rejected the conscious coquetry of his later works.

When the play was to be performed in 1908, at the Intimate Theater, Strindberg gave the following instructions to Anna Flygare, who was to play the leading role: "Eros is not the dominant theme. Eros here only symbolizes *caritas*, that great love which bears all things, endures all things, forgives all things, which hopes and believes even when all things fail. Better expressed in the stepmother's transformation, and best in the final scene: Love stronger than death!"

Strindberg's peculiarly sublimated poet's love (for Harriet Bosse), its power in his dreams and his imagination when they were apart, and its vulnerability and helplessness when they were together every day—these are the foundations of the dramatic fairy tale of the young duchess Swanwhite. She loves the young prince and the prince loves her; her diabolical stepmother persecutes her, and the dissolute young king pays court to her. Her beloved drowns, but she regains him through her compassion and purity.

The fairy play achieves balance by the author's skill in matching the often rather cloying exchanges between Swanwhite and her lover with rejoinders by the stepmother, and at times the young king, that are several shades more earthy than is usual in fairy tales.

Touches of a highly sophisticated chiaroscuro world such as we find in Maeterlinck, hot but carefully controlled sensuality, decorative figures in the pre-Raphaelite manner, and with it all the mood of a crystalline Swedish morning among the islands—all this reads like a daring mixture of heterogeneous elements, but on the stage it fuses simply into a fairy tale painted in strong, clear colors. At times the stylized formulations rise to solemn lyrical prose.

CARL XII
(1901)

In midsummer 1901, Strindberg completed *Carl XII*. His choice of theme was in some ways astounding. Since the publication of his book *The Swedish People* (1882) he was resented throughout the country for his hatred of Carl XII. Thus there is little likelihood that it was out of admiration that he began to study the character of a man whom he considered "Sweden's destroyer, the great criminal, the ruffian, idol of rowdies, counterfeiter." In his *Open Letter to the Intimate Theater*, Strindberg gave a further explanation of his choice by stating that "every criminal has the right to defend himself." At bottom, the author, like it or not, felt a certain admiration for the King. Not because Carl was supposed to have been a man of genius, for Strindberg thought him simpleminded and petty. Nor was it because Carl had been a strong-willed man, for Strindberg thought of him as obsessively stubborn and abnormally ambitious. No—Strindberg chose his hero because Carl XII was a powerful personality, solitary, unhappy, original, and distrustful of women. What interested Strindberg most was how the King had met his death, and this is the event he set out to describe in the play.

The King perishes "in his battle against the powers, himself already ruined by disharmonies that have come to light and doubts that have been aroused." The series of misfortunes that befall the King are the consequence of his own arrogance which prompts him to take upon himself the role of providence. Nor is the King capable of authentic guilt feelings: "I only defended myself, my country, my royal inheritance!"

The drama of the "criminal" Carl XII is one of Strindberg's most personal history dramas. His own experience paralleled that of the King who, after long years spent abroad, comes ashore in Schonen and settles down in Lund. Like him, Strindberg had come to Schonen, after his *Inferno* experiences in Paris and in Austria, and had taken up residence in Lund, in the Grönegatan, only a few steps from the house where Carl XII had established his residence from 1716 to 1718. And he had had the same feelings as the King, "who does not dare return to his homeland because he is ashamed of his failure."

In formal structure, the piece differs sharply from *The Folkung Saga* and *Gustav Vasa*, both packed with action in the Shakespearean manner. On the surface, there is little action in *Carl XII*. Almost the entire piece takes place in a mood of oppressive expectancy, a waiting for the shot that finally rings out in Fredriksten Fortress. The play gives the impression of a musical composition scored in a minor key, with theme and variations, a dream-play revival of the venerable dramatic genre from Swedish history. The events that occur between that windy December morning in 1715 when the king, pale and shivering with cold, sets foot on Swedish soil, and that mystery-shrouded deadly shot in Norway, are described in highly concentrated mood-effects. Just as in *Gustav Vasa,* our interest in the King grows with every stroke of the pen. The central figure is seen closely only in the second act. The scenes are short, the dialogue often clipped and laconic. Storm, rain, and racing clouds play a relentless game with the human characters. The inspiration that joins dialogue to dialogue reminds us not so much of other dramatists as of Beethoven, for whom Strindberg in the years after the *Inferno* period felt profound admiration, and whose sonatas he at times called his models in the composition of his plays.

To Damascus, Part III
(*Till Damaskus III,* 1901)

During rehearsals for the première of *To Damascus, Part I,* in November of 1900 at the Dramatic Theater in Stockholm, Strindberg had fallen in love with Harriet Bosse, who was playing the role of the "lady." This seems to have been the time when he conceived the idea of a third part. On February 8, 1901, he noted that he was working on this third part; and when he wrote his last will, on September 16, he mentioned the manuscript of *Part III* (apparently finished by then) as part of his estate.

At the beginning of the play, The Unknown stands at the foot of a mighty mountain on whose peak the monastery, goal of his travels, gleams chalk white in the sun. Even this last stage of his road is beset with difficulties. First, he takes leave of his half-grown daughter—a task which turns out to be much less painful than he had feared. More difficult, however, is his final leave-taking from his wife. Indeed, he returns once more to the terrestrial level, and marries her a second time.

But before long the two marriage partners have a falling-out, on which The Unknown makes some spirited comments in his dialogue with his baser self, the Tempter. The "lady" takes leave for good, and goes on her way; and in the final scene, The Unknown can at last enter into the higher sphere of the (nondenominational) monastery.

This third part of the trilogy contains even more epic digressions than did the second. There are enchanting poetic parts, many brilliant ideas, but only a few dramatic highpoints.

In the first part, The Unknown had been portrayed as one who utterly distrusts everything. Then came the paradox: he distrusted his own distrust. It, too, was exposed as fraud; and faith in God's wise governance could be sensed in the background. In the first two parts it became evident that certain illusions—of wealth, honor, power, and love—were still holding sway, their power unbroken. But after this entry into the monastery, The Unknown has overcome the last temptations of this world. The result of his long journey and ardent quest is resignation and faith in the Eternal and the realm of humanity. Here is a consistent and worthy conclusion to the court trial in which Strindberg had passed judgment upon himself.

ENGELBREKT
(1901)

On August 8, 1901 Strindberg began working on his drama about Engelbrekt, Swedish freedom fighter of the fifteenth century. On the next day, a doctor reported to him that a new member of the family was on the way. On August 22, Strindberg made this note: "Woke up without much interest in the *Engelbrekt* on which I am working." On that same day, he further noted that he received a letter from his wife "in which she announced that she had left me for good." September 1: "Terrible to live, alone!" And two days later: "Letter from Harriet! *Engelbrekt* finished!" The drama had been finished in a mood of utter dejection. It is extraordinarily uninspired; the dialogue lacks both luster and pace. Just as with *Gustav Adolf*, the effort involved in achieving historical accuracy contributed to the flagging of Strindberg's imagination.

It would seem that Strindberg himself liked *Engelbrekt*. In his youth, he had been a supporter of the Scandinavian idea; later on, he came to oppose the "Dovre-oldsters" Ibsen and Björnson. Now he was newly married to a Norwegian woman whose father was a German and whose brother was a cadet in the Norwegian army. Strindberg had spent the month of July with Harriet in Denmark, were the couple attended the Union Day celebrations. It was no simple matter for the author of a Swedish historical drama to be married to a Norwegian. The Union between Sweden and Norway had entered a crisis which, in November of 1905, was to end in the separation of the two countries. For the newly married Strindberg, it may have been important to pay tribute to the memory of Engelbrekt, who could be both a good Swedish patriot and at the same time a supporter of the Kalmar Union.

CHRISTINA
(*Kristina*, 1901)

No sooner had he finished *Engelbrekt* than Strindberg began work on *Christina*, one of his most entertaining pieces.

Christina is totally unhistorical. Of all the many plays written around that queen, this one is most like a lampoon. But it is a colorful and diabolical description of a woman which stands on its own artistic merit. Christina herself, despite her levity, is a living human being. Strindberg's portrayal of the famous queen turned into a satire done with elegance, nimbleness, and many points of high merit.

Christina's entrance in the first act, in Riddarholms Church, is the stage entrance of a prima donna at the head of her devoted troupe. In the course of the action, she plays diverse roles, varying according to her situation and her partners. She treats her former favorite Magnus Gabriel de la Gardie, now in disgrace, cajolingly, like a cat—who suddenly shows her claws. With Holm the tailor she acts majestic and masterful, but in the presence of old Axel Oxenstierna, her chancellor, she is "little Kerstin" (tiny Tina) who stammers childish prattle and pretends innocence. To the Spanish ambassador Pimentelli, she presents herself as the fiery lover, with daring intimacy and burning glances—but for Klas Tott, with whom she falls seriously in love, she changes into a "graceful woman soft in nature, with languishing demeanor." She loves to be surrounded by men—on their knees.

All the time she remains the actress whose stage is the Swedish throne. Strindberg himself emphasized that he had written the role for Harriet Bosse, "the only person who can play it." (*Christina* was indeed one of Harriet Bosse's outstanding roles.) Obviously, the role was to an important extent also a portrayal of Miss Bosse herself. Strindberg wrote to her: ". . . even though I always knew who you were, your nature, your inclinations—in *Christina* I have *explained* it all!"

The piece deals with a headstrong queen who plays games with power, with money, and with men, but finally becomes herself the plaything of powerful passions. When Queen Christina tops her lavish waste and system of favorites by precipitating the country into war with Bremen, the underlying corruption is exposed in a lampooning pamphlet; disturbances break out in Stockholm, and Christina is compelled to abdicate. However, in the final scene, she shows signs of greatness and displays that intellectual superiority which the audience had all along suspected lay underneath her deportment.

A Dream Play
(Ett drömspel, 1901)

A Dream Play seems to have been started in September of 1901, and to have been completed about November 20. (The *Prologue*—a dialogue between Indra and his daughter high up in the clouds—was added five years later.) On November 18, Strindberg wrote in his diary the following lines that tie directly into the drama's final scenes:

Am reading about the teachings of the Indian religion.—The whole world purely an illusion. . . . The divine archpower . . . let itself be seduced by Maja or the urge of procreation. The divine archmatter thereby committed a sin against itself (love is sin; this is why the torment of love is the worst hell there is). The world thus exists purely because of a sin, if indeed it does exist—for it is merely a vision seen in a dream (thus my *Dream Play* an image of life), a phantom whose destruction is the task of asceticism. But that task is at odds with the urge to love, and the final result is an incessant vacillation between the turmoil of the flesh and penitential torment!—That seems to be the solution to the riddle of the world!—I discovered the foregoing in the history of literature, just when I had intended to conclude the dream play *The Growing Castle.* That was on the 18th, in the morning. But on that morning I saw the castle (=the barracks of the Horse Guards) as if it were bathed in the light of the rising sun.—Now the "Indian religion" has given me the explanation of my dream play, and of the meaning of Indra's daughter, the secret of the Door=Nothingness.—All day I read about Buddhism.

Another stimulus to write *A Dream Play*, besides the "Indian religion," was Harriet Bosse's unusual beauty, which had captivated Strindberg from the start. Her face, with its slightly almond-shaped brown eyes and jet-black hair, had a mysterious Oriental radiance. Strindberg wrote the role of Indra's daughter for her, and during the writing he decorated his home with Indian draperies. Harriet had returned to him for good, and was now living with him. Rarely had there been a time when he was more at peace with a woman and with life than during this period. But the feeling of peace had an admixture of sorrow, it was overly charged with the awareness of all that is evil and ugly and tragic, all that is irrevocably bound up with the human condition.

At bottom, *A Dream Play* turned into a kind of *To Damascus, Part IV*. The motto *resignation* has here changed to the password *compassion*. In his "earlier *Dream Play*," as he called *To Damascus* in the foreword, Strindberg had appeared as The Unknown, the beggar, and the Tempter. In *A Dream Play* he again appears in three incarnations—the officer, the advocate, and the poet. By characterizing his new view of life as a dream play, he relieved himself of the necessity to give much thought to the logical connections between the uneven scenes. The leading character was in his mind; so were the settings; the play's basic mood was given and, finally, the characteristics of the fairy play were as usable here as in the earlier dramas of man's journey. The plan for *A Dream Play* was taking shape in his imagination.

Strindberg takes Indra's daughter on a dream-journey and leads her to the imprisoned officer in the strange growing castle, to the worldly-wise woman who is doorkeeper at the opera house, and to the man whose job it is to put up posters and whose greatest desire is to own a green boat and a seining net. Indra's daughter observes the officer waiting for the singer Miss Victoria until his hair turns grey, his rose bouquet is withered. She goes through the prosaic day-to-day routine of marriage with the advocate, and tries to console him for his failure to obtain a promotion. After he has achieved the honor of a doctoral degree, she must witness his return to the schooldesk, and his inability to reckon even two times two. After an excursion to the Riviera, where she finds herself revolted by the contrast between the proletarian misery of the coal carriers and the luxury of the wealthy, she comes to Fingal's Cave, and there, alone with the poet, she listens to the lament of the wind and the waves. When the mystical door at the opera house is thrown open, she sees the learned representatives of four academic faculties in arduous disagreement over the most basic problems of human knowledge. The poet presents her with a writ that lists the grievances of suffering mankind, and she shakes the dust of the earth from her feet to enter the growing castle. At the moment when the flames swallow the castle's roof, there appears "a wall of human faces, questioning, sorrowful, in despair," and the budding blossom on the roof bursts open into a gigantic chrysanthemum.

Despite its excess of fantasy and imagination, the play, on closer study, reveals a rich content of solid reality to those who are familiar with the Stockholm of that day, and with Strindberg's own family situation. Still, it is instructive to observe the skill with which he managed to transform concrete facts into poetic fiction. In his foreword, he says:

> Following my earlier dream play *To Damascus*, I have tried to imitate the incoherent yet seemingly logical structure of the dream. Anything can happen, anything is possible and probable. Time and space do not exist. From a few puny facts, the imagination takes wing and traces new patterns: a mixture of memories, experiences, inventions, improbabilities, and improvisations. . . . As to the loose, incoherent form, it, too, is so only in appearance. On closer scrutiny, we can see its rather firm composition—a symphony, polyphonic, cemented here and there with the recurrent main motif repeated and varied in every key by its more than thirty voices.

Both Strindberg's foreword to *A Dream Play* and his techniques in structuring the drama give evidence of his knowledge of the peculiarities of the dream, a knowledge which surely did not stem entirely from personal experience but must also have been based firmly on the scientific investigations of his time.

The first scene after the *Prologue* offers an example. The stage shows a forest of gigantic roses in resplendent colors; beyond can be seen the guilded roof of the growing castle. This introductory scene is well known to scientific dream analysts. It exhibits characteristics typical of the so-called image stage, immediately preceding the moment when the dreamer falls asleep. At that moment, the sleeper often sees stylized plants in colorful splendor. At first they are images, but then contact is lost with the ego, which is half outside observer, and suddenly we are within the strange landscape we had observed.

The well-known transformation of things in a dream—the door that turns suddenly into a cabinet, the linden tree which becomes a clothes rack—is documented in the scientific literature of Strindberg's time (including especially Freud's famous *Interpretation of Dreams*). Doubtless, Strindberg understood that a presentation of dream pictures without intelligible connection would have little appeal to the public. Accordingly, he produced a sequence of scenes which had logic and a basic theme even while retaining certain suggestive peculiarities of the dream. This forced him to depart in some respects from the customary model of the dream. His purpose was to show how two-faced life is—the lovely flower has its roots in dirty soil, the whispering waves draw the ship into the depths. *A Dream Play* is a journey in a waking dream.

Gustav III
(1902)

After his portrayal in *Christina* of the play actress on the Swedish throne, Strindberg was also bound to present a portrait of the crowned play actor in Swedish history. He completed *Gustav III* on March 16, 1902, one hundred and ten years to the day after the attack on the King's life at a masquerade in the Stockholm opera house. Strindberg himself took care to note this fact.

Strindberg seized with enthusiasm on the dramatic moments in Gustav III's life, and on the ambiance of espionage and counterespionage surrounding the throne. The play describes the intrigues that preceded the meeting of the Diet in 1789, when the King with the support of the bourgeoisie was planning a coup that would substantially extend his powers. The first act, in Holmsberg's bookstore, informs us of the festering conflict between King and nobility. The second act, notable for its brilliant verbal duels, shows us the King at close range, so to speak. The third act presents the conspiracy of the nobles; and the fourth act, adroitly increasing the tension, shows the opposing factions face to face at a public festivity.

Strindberg was primarily interested in the King's character, and he appraised it with fair objectivity. He was convinced he understood that character, though he evinced a trace of contempt for what he considered the impersonal manner of actors. Even in those early days when Strindberg had intended to become an actor, he thought, as he expressed it in *The Son of the Servant*, that "It looked as though, at bottom, the actor did not need to understand anything, as long as it sounded good." Two marriages with actresses had given him further opportunities to study the minds of professional actors. They possessed overwhelming charm; but in his hours of bitterness their souls looked to him like a blank sheet of paper which different men

and women covered with various texts. Yet Strindberg, himself fickle, allowed himself to be captivated
by actors' rapidly changing personalities. However
acid his comments on their psychic life, he nevertheless remains their admirer—just like the officer
in *A Dream Play* who waits, fading rose bouquet in
hand, until his hair has turned snow white.

Something of this ambivalent attitude is discerni-
ble in Strindberg's portrayal of Gustav III, a splendid specimen in his gallery of historical portraits.
The King is neither profound nor particularly
original, but he is an extremely gifted performer.
In his audience room in Haga Castle, on the wall
facing his desk, there hangs a mirror in which he
studies his own attitudes and poses. When he is
setting out for the province of Dalarna to raise an
army, his most serious concern is to secure for himself the Dalecarlian national costume. He is an actor
who plays the leading role in the great drama of
power over Sweden, and even does so *con amore*,
intelligently, playfully, but is fundamentally un-
affected and untouchable.

But there are several scenes, between the King
and Queen and between the Secretary of State
Schröderheim and his beautiful wife, in which the
portrayal assumes depth in the highly personal,
typically Strindbergian manner. When the issue was
marital conflicts in matters of love, Strindberg's
powers to project himself into the man's situation
and to plead his case were well-nigh inexhaustible.
The perfumed Gustav III and the laconic and brutal
Charles XII reeking of the stables were equally
close to Strindberg's heart when they confronted
that most formidable enemy: woman.

THE HOLLANDER
(*Holländaren*, 1902)

Strindberg's unfinished play *The Hollander* is a highly personal dramatic poem about the love and hate of woman. Cast in the form of a dream play and giving an intimation of Strindberg's future chamber plays, the piece tells the dramatic story of a descendant of the captain of the *Flying Dutchman* whose ship founders near a coastal town. The Hollander himself is saved and brought ashore. In a dream, his mother appears to him, and he bares his heart to her: "I cannot understand why love, heaven's gift, should open the gates of hell; I cannot understand how it is possible that a she-demon comes toward me and I see an angel?" His views of the female sex are based on rich experience: The Hollander has gone through six divorces! But he has barely laid eyes on young Lilith in her bridal gown when he is overcome by her beauty and woos her with an enthusiastic hymn. In Act Two they get married, despite the eloquent warning of his apprentice and servant Ukko. In the third act, the unhappiness of happiness begins: "You fill my life, and still it is empty!" We hear the discordant notes of irritation, contempt, hate. She leaves him, and he is alone once more.

It seems probable that Strindberg had intended to expose Lilith's dubious morality, and let the Hollander go back to sea in the fourth act. But he lost interest and did not continue. On July 19, he made up with Harriet Bosse, and on the following day he wrote to her: "What a wonderful day, yesterday! A happy day for the Hollander!" And so the "fragment" got its proper ending, even though the final rejoinder remained unwritten. The reason *The Hollander* was not completed, and was never published, is that once again, peace had broken out between Strindberg and Harriet Bosse.

THE NIGHTINGALE IN WITTENBERG
(*Näktergalen i Wittenberg*, 1903)

A number of theatrical failures in Sweden —with *Easter*, *Midsummer*, and *Engelbrekt*—had made stage directors very cautious. Strindberg encountered difficulties in placing his plays. *The Hollander* remained unfinished, as did "a first scene-outline for a dramatic saga in five acts" entitled *Homunculus* (1902), which did not seem promising enough to warrant further work. Strindberg had begun a sequel to the *Damascus* series under the title *Walpurgis Night on Fagervik* (*Valborgsafton pa Fagervik*), which takes The Unknown to Fagervik where he engages in a song contest with a Scald; Strindberg now cut the work up and made it into a cycle of poems under the title *Night of the Trinity*.

He then turned back to history. He took a special interest in German history, because his plays seemed to be held in higher esteem in Germany than in his native Sweden. He began to look for a German theme attractive to a German audience. The figure of the reformer Luther greatly interested him; indeed, it seemed to him at times that he and Luther were brothers in spirit. He felt himself drawn most strongly to the German reformer, whom he saw as a great solitary proudly defying worldly power and public opinion. "Alone! All the better! Now, great Living God, it is just we alone: you and I!" Luther is made to say after he is released from his monastic vows and has given up his friends. Strindberg could have said the same words in his own behalf when he wrote *The Nightingale in Wittenberg.*

The drama with this ironical title lets us accompany "the biggest mouth in Germany" on a broadly conceived chronological procession, from his controversies in his parental home, through the unfortunate times in the cloister, and on to the nailing of the famous theses to the church door in Wittenberg; and from there to the Diet of Worms, and the secluded room in the Wartburg.

Despite the play's length, we never feel that we are getting closer to its principal character. Strindberg had critical admiration for his hero but did not get inside his mind. The description is chopped up into numerous short scenes. At intervals, Strindberg amused himself by making the great figures of cultural history pass in review: Erasmus, Ulrich von Hutten, Hans Sachs, Lucas Cranach, Philip Melanchthon. Even Doctor Faustus is drawn in. In a letter of May 1904 Strindberg called this work his "best, most beautiful, and perhaps final drama."

So far, his judgment of his own piece has not been borne out. The play's superficially drawn characters, the hectic chase through fourteen sets, the multitude of minor figures, and the lack of a truly dramatic development make its performance difficult. Even radical abridgments do not seem to give it power. Once again it turned out that the more thoroughly Strindberg prepared himself for an his-

torical drama, the more difficult it became for him
to breathe life into it. The scholar's ambition clipped
the wings of the poet's imagination.

Moses
(*Genom öknar till arvland, eller Moses,*
1903)

Strindberg did not content himself with
the Luther drama as a slice of world history. He
seems to have turned to his next play immediately
on completing *The Nightingale in Wittenberg.* He
intended to proceed methodically, and now revived
a monumental plan he had conceived earlier. He
was envisioning a gigantic historical cycle consist-
ing of at least three trilogies of five-act plays, of
which *The Nightingale in Wittenberg* was to be
one. He wrote three shorter pieces around the
central figures of Moses, Socrates, and Christ. After
that, he lost interest. (In the same way, his am-
bitiously conceived attempt to write a "drama of
old Nordic saga," *Starkodder Skald,* to which in the
spring of 1906 he added a prologue in verse, did
not go beyond a first sketch, and is preserved only
as a fragment.)

The first drama in the historical cycle, *Through
the Wilderness to the Promised Land,* or *Moses,* is
a superficially regrouped paraphrase of the Bible
story of Moses leading the people of Israel from
Egypt through the deserts to the land of Canaan.
The artificially archaic dialogue of the twenty-one
scenes reminds us of the clumsy yet endearing Bible
plays of the age of the Reformation.

HELLAS, OR SOCRATES
(*Hellas, eller Sokrates*, 1903)

Play number two in the "historical series" was begun, according to Strindberg's diary, in mid-October, and completed within the week. The piece deals with the same declining Hellas as did Strindberg's youthful drama *Hermione*, but it lacks a genuinely dramatic plot. Through nineteen scenes, we hear Socrates, Pericles, Protagoras, Plato, Phidias, Euripides, and other famous men hold forth on politics, religion, and woman. It is noticeable, however, that Strindberg is here somewhat more deeply involved than he was in his *Moses*.

Strindberg felt a special sympathy for Euripides —who was a sort of Strindberg of antiquity—and he despised Aristophanes as heartily as he did the comedy writers of his own time. But his strongest sympathy went out to Socrates, with whom he felt in harmony because of Socrates' critical view of woman and of marriage. Thus the world-famous sage, before emptying the poisonous cup in the final scene, is given ample opportunity to hurl verbal poisoned darts of the best Strindbergian invective at his Xanthippe.

CHRIST
(*Lammet och vilddjuret, eller Christus*, 1903)

The third "historical" drama, *The Lamb and the Wild Beast*, or *Christ*, was begun about October 19, according to Strindberg's diary, and

completed on November 5, 1903. Its original title
was *Messiah and Anti-Messiah*. Strindberg had been
planning since 1870 to write a play about Jesus of
Nazareth: here, then, was the result.

The colors are more garish than in the two
preceding plays. The play begins with a description
of the "Lamb" Christ, from his birth in Bethlehem
to his death on Golgotha. Christ himself does not
appear, he is merely spoken about. Golgotha is ef-
fectively presented in symbolic form—the shadows
of three crosses seen upon white chalk cliffs. The
action shifts from Jerusalem to Rome, where we are
presented, one after the other, with three bestial
figures—Caligula, Claudius, and Nero. Nero falls
under the daggers of his slaves, and thus the Lamb
is victorious. The wandering Jew Cartaphilos acts
as the recurring figure tying the scenes together.

Some of the scenes show Strindberg in better
control than he had been in his earlier "world-
historical" plays. Caiaphas' interrogation of John
before the Great Council is highly effective, because John's replies throughout the entire dialogue
move on an altogether different plane than Caiaphas'
questions. The scenes of the mad Caligula adoring
his own image, and of Nero lost in the catacombs,
surely have a certain dramatic power.

THE THUNDERSTORM
(*Oväder*, 1907)

In the fall of 1906, the twenty-four-year
old stage director August Falck went on a sensational tour with *Miss Julie*, for which he at least

earned an incontestable success, even on the stage of the People's Theater in Stockholm. The event prompted Strindberg to revive an old project: to establish a theater of his own. His plans became more concrete after a meeting with Falck late in 1906. The first rumors of the project appeared in the Stockholm press as early as December of that year.

The format of the plays that would be suitable for performance in an intimate theater began to take ever clearer shape in Strindberg's mind. "The secret program" for the repertory of a Strindberg Theater would have to be "the transposition of the idea of chamber music into drama." "The intimate procedure, the significant motif, painstaking execution," as he expressed it in his "Memorandum to the Members of the Intimate Theater." Even before he had finished his first chamber play, he defined the limits still more rigorously in a letter to Adolf Paul: "A small motif, treated in detail, a small cast, large issues, free imagination but based on observation, experience carefully examined, simple but not too simple, no large apparatus, no unnecessary minor characters, no regular five-acters or 'old saws,' no pieces lasting the whole evening."

But what about the themes? Strindberg, on January 25, 1907, noted: "Thunderstorm, snowstorm. Write *Thunderstorm*." On February 13, he informed Falck that the first chamber play was ready. Despite the title (*Oväder* literally means bad weather), the action takes place in an unusually calm atmosphere, on a summer's evening in Stockholm's fashionable quarter, Östermalm.

Strindberg's alter ego, the Gentleman, is looking forward to spending his declining years in comfort. He has talks with the baker, and plays chess with his brother. "No love, no friends—just a little company in one's solitude; then men become men, without any mutual claims to feelings and sympathies." Still, this calm and solitude weigh on him; he is expecting something to happen.

Something does happen. A less cultured man moves into the apartment upstairs with his wife and young daughter and opens a gambling club; there are nightly orgies. In the end he vanishes into thin air, and we learn what he has left behind: the Gentleman's own former wife, and their daughter. Before the two move out, the Gentleman has an abrasive confrontation with the woman, though this gives him an opportunity, under the pretense of compassion, to make agreeable comparisons between himself and her vanished second husband.

A slight thunderstorm, followed by a mild shower, accompanies the evening's events. At the end the air is clear, and the first street lamp of the season lights up. Now the Gentleman can withdraw into his isolation with even fewer scruples than before: the one and only link that had still bound him to others—the memory of his wife and child—has proved to be tarnished. The circle of the drama is closed: the last flare-up of passion dies in the ashes of old age.

Strindberg spent the summer of 1906 in his apartment in Ostermalm. His principal visitor was his brother Axel, who dropped in on occasion to play some Beethoven for him. On July 17, Strindberg reported that the street lights had been lit the night before for the first time. In a draft version, he called the play The First Lantern (Första lyktan); two weeks later, he reported significantly: "Today,

August 2, finally the ideal weather: thunder and rain. I can breathe."

The actual "bad weather," obviously, was centered in Harriet Bosse. Strindberg had every reason to assume that his young, beautiful, and popular former wife would marry again, and he was afraid that their little daughter Anne-Marie would have a stepfather. In *The Thunderstorm* he meant to give a warning to Harriet Bosse, just as he once had tried to warn Siri von Essen with *Creditors*.

After the Fire
(*Brända tomten*, 1907)

August Falck reported that one morning in Stockholm, while taking a walk with Strindberg, they passed a house in which Strindberg had lived on three different occasions. The house had burned down the night before. "We stopped. Strindberg put his hand on my arm and pointed to the yard. In a split second, he had grasped the dramatic effect of a defoliated apple tree whose buds had opened during the fire: and now in all the soot and desolation, they seemed a revelation." To judge by his diary, Strindberg had the idea for the chamber play *After the Fire* as early as January 1907; his first title for it was *The World Weaver*. He finished the play in early March.

After the Fire describes how the poet's alter ego, the Stranger, returns to his home in Sweden and finds the house of his birth lying in ashes. While he stumbles about among the ruins, memories come back to him. But they are not cheerful memories.

In conversations with his brother, who is a dyer, and with a painter, a stone mason, a student, and other inhabitants, so much derogatory information emerges that in the end The Unknown is convinced that the house had been a den of crime and depravity. He even suspects that his brother the dyer had set the fire and then put the blame on the student, who is the lover of the dyer's wife. After the inquiry, the Stranger wanders away "out into the wide world," poorer by a few sentimental illusions.

At bottom, the piece is one continuous quarrelsome debunking of sentimental notions about the "house of my birth." With all its naturalistic precision, it is something of a dream play. The Stranger, Strindberg, saw people and things as if in a dream turned upside down. He retained the dream vision but did not take that dream too seriously. Meanwhile, he was waiting for the end—and for the last great exposure which would show that life was no more than an evil dream.

As a stage play, *After the Fire* belongs among Strindberg's most difficult masterpieces. The substance of the conflict is beclouded by many meditations and digressions. Actually, it is a crime play— murderous arson, and then a sleuth playing Sherlock Holmes among the ashes. But the suspense is weakened by the fact that the Stranger is not much interested in discovering the culprit. Instead, he becomes involved in lengthy disquisitions on the imperfections of the human race—disquisitions which, for all their quarrelsomeness, at times rise to visionary poetry of a peculiar beauty.

THE GHOST SONATA
(*Spöksonaten*, 1907)

In Strindberg's third chamber play, his revulsion and horror, his contempt for life and all mankind, becomes transmuted into a monumental fantasy. His diary and letters give evidence of violent fluctuations in his creative mood. This much is certain: the spring of 1907 was an unusually grim period in his private life. Fortunately, his creative energy does not seem to have suffered—on the contrary, he succeeded in·raising the trivialities of daily life up to a dream realm where they assumed convincing character.

The two first acts of *The Ghost Sonata* are an exposure of the inhabitants of an upper-class apartment house in Stockholm. An army colonel with a noble name lives on the ground floor. However, his military rank is overstated, his noble name an error, and his daughter is not his daughter. When his wig and his dentures are removed, his moustache shaved off, and his metal corset is unlaced, we see before us an ex-butler. The woman to whom he is married was a great beauty in bygone days. Her youthful beauty is preserved in a white marble sculpture. But now she has shriveled up like a mummy, and likes to sit inside a closet because her eyes cannot bear daylight. The daughter, who prefers to stay in the hyacinth room among the flowers, is fading away in sickness.

The daughter's real father, the mummy's former lover, is a wealthy crippled octogenarian named Hummel, who is moved about in a wheelchair. On one occasion he practices ostentatious charity—on another he interferes with the lives of others in vampire fashion. He comes to call on the colonel for the "usual ghost supper." Besides the colonel's family, there are present the mentally unbalanced canoness Beate von Holsteinkrona and Baron Skanskorg, whom Hummel addresses as "the jewel thief." Usually, these pillars of society "drink tea, say not a word, or the colonel alone speaks; and then they nibble cookies, all together, like mice in the attic." But when Hummel is in attendance, there is no tea and no conversation. Instead, Hummel brutally exposes "this lovely home where beauty, culture, and affluence converge."

Then comes what failed to happen in *After the Fire*—the exposure of the exposer himself. The Mummy throws a sudden fit of rationality. We learn that Hummel has deceived her with false promises, that he has blackmailed a consul, and that later he practiced usury in Hamburg, where he threatened a young girl who witnessed one of his crimes. Old Hummel, who during the procedure has sunk deeper and deeper in his chair, begins to cackle like a parrot. He is moved into the closet and a Japanese screen is put up in front of it: the "death screen," which is brought out whenever there is a death in the family.

The lives of the young people, too, are poisoned. During that macabre supper, a love scene between the colonel's daughter and the student takes place in the hyacinth room, under the eyes of a Buddha image. The two ethereal personalities meet in their common enthusiasm for flowers—but the young woman dies because her health has been undermined from birth.

Strindberg first intended to call the piece *Ghost*

Supper, but after making several important changes he decided on *The Ghost Sonata*. The title refers to Beethoven's D-minor piano sonata, of which Strindberg was especially fond. This key was wholly in harmony with his somber state of mind at that period.

In *The Ghost Sonata*, even more emphatically than in *The Dance of Death*, Strindberg depicts life as a nightmare. The milkmaid is the embodiment of Hummel's bad conscience, just as the decapitated sailor is the conscience of the Judge in *Advent*. Hummel, puffing himself up while he exposes the colonel's family, resembles the poison-tongued step-mother in *Swanwhite*; and when he gets his re-buttal, he collapses just as Adolf does in *Creditors*. The kindly and jovial student wanders about like a male reincarnation of Eleonora in *Easter*. He sees things that are hidden, and suffers with those who are in distress. At the same time, like the Stranger in *After the Fire*, and like Strindberg himself, he is obsessed by a desire to speak the truth bluntly. As a model of expressionistic drama and its technique, *The Ghost Sonata* is of importance the world over, especially in Germany. Its influence on O'Neill, Pirandello, Ionesco, and Adamov is unmistakable.

THE ISLAND OF THE DEAD
(*Fragment*, 1907)

On April 15, 1907 Strindberg noted in his diary: "My mind has of late been occupied with death and what lies beyond. Yesterday, read Plato's *Timaeus* and *Phaido*. Should like to know whether

I must die now, or soon. Am currently working on *Island of the Dead*, in which I describe the awakening after death, and what comes after, but I shy away, with a shudder, from laying bare the abysmal misery of life." Arnold Böcklin's famous painting *The Island of the Dead* (*Toten-Insel*) had fascinated Strindberg as it had so many of his contemporaries. Earlier, Strindberg had ended *The Ghost Sonata* by having Böcklin's painting appear on the backdrop, while the room on stage is fading out to the accompaniment of soft funereal music. He now mixed his impressions of the painting with Swedenborgian visions. In his *Bluebook*, he has described for us his dream of paradise, inspired by both *The Island of the Dead* and Swedenborg. It was this vision of life after death to which he tried to give dramatic form in the rather unprepossessing fragment *The Island of the Dead*, or, as he also called it, *Hades*.

A teacher has died and is received on the Island of the Dead. In the second scene, under the name Assir, he learnedly converses "in a white Egyptian room" with the Sage about the "curious web" of his life. In the course of the conversation his character is analyzed. Strindberg has outlined only the setting of the third scene. Assir, "rejuvenated and in bright garments," sits on a bench near the shore among green trees; a gentle wind is blowing and waves splash softly. In the background can be seen the opposite shore, with an orange grove and a white marble temple. Here the fragment stops.

On April 26, Strindberg informed Emil Schering: "I had started on a great chamber play about [Böcklin's] Island of the Dead. The beginning was good, but I lost interest, just as I have lost interest in life and can feel the end approaching."

Strindberg's experience with his sister Anna, who was then keeping house for him, provided the stimulus for this work. She was slovenly, he meticulous. Besides, he was in physical pain and easily upset. To make a long story short, Anna had enough and left without a warning. "You'll be sorry!" Strindberg is supposed to have hissed after her. His first act of revenge seems to have been *The Bloody Hand* (*Den blödande handen*), a play which he burned. The second was *The Island of the Dead*, the third *The Pelican* (*Pelikanen*), a general settling of accounts. In the fragment *The Island of the Dead*, he brought his sister on stage under her own name, portraying her as the quarrelsome and slatternly schoolmaster's wife.

THE PELICAN
(*Pelikanen*, 1907)

Strindberg's bitterness toward his once beloved sister Anna seems to have risen to a pitch of fury as a combined result of his physical pain and his displeasure with her housekeeping. Though she had always loyally stood by his side, he now wanted nothing more to do with her—in fact, he never wanted to see her again.

His fury inspired him to write a drama about a demoniacal mother. Like Alice in *The Dance of Death* and the Mummy in *The Ghost Sonata*, she is drawn in superhuman proportions: a grotesque animal, similar to a female pelican. We can readily imagine what life with her must have been like for her unfortunate husband! But she deserves our pity too. Her malice is so enormous, so much like a curse, that she is bound to arouse the audience's compassion. From such responses and visions was the play about the pelican born. Strindberg's sister Anna inspired some of the darkest compositions drawn from her brother's world of fantasy.

This play constitutes Strindberg's ultimate dissection of the female mind. The victim whose corrupt inner life is here exposed to view is the widow of the schoolmaster whom we have met in *The Island of the Dead*. While her depravity is revealed more and more completely as the action unrolls, the character of her dead husband, so misunderstood in life, assumes ever greater nobility and purity in the minds of their son and daughter. The father had left behind a letter to his son in which he described his wife's worst faults. She had stolen household money, padded the bills, purchased bad merchandise at excessive prices; she herself ate a good meal in the kitchen, before noon, and then fed her children with leftovers. She took the cream off the milk, and embezzled the money for heating fuel so that the family had to sit in the cold. She had an affair with Axel, lieutenant in the reserves. She lent him money, and he married her daughter. The children grew up poorly fed and tired of life. Finally the son bursts out: "I despise life, mankind, society, and myself so totally that I don't even want to take the trouble to live." Drunk, he sets fire to the house; the mother leaps out the window and perishes in the flames. Brother and sister, dying, fall into each other's arms, raving of their final liberation: "Now come the summer vacations!"

The Pelican is a fearsome play, a raging study of malice and degeneracy, darkly fascinating and horrifying, until it slips, almost imperceptively, into absurdity, the disproportions of a grotesque. Though Strindberg was in part driven by private motives—repentance and revenge—the piece has passages of sublime originality and an artistic strength of purpose that overcome all our reservations. The author's conviction that he himself is subject to the same judgment as his characters lends to each scene a sense of fateful urgency and human solidarity that must grip any audience. All that is ugly and base assumes in this play a character of unreality.

The nightmarish mood, the sharply drawn characters (especially the mother), the finely pointed dialogue, and the effective conception of *The Pelican* have made it, next to *The Ghost Sonata*, Strindberg's most frequently staged chamber play. It is, however, extremely difficult to perform successfully. The play can slip away into ridiculous farce with an uncanny ease, if the dream atmosphere is not firmly brought out. In this respect, *The Pelican*—with its dead men who walk, its living people who assume animal shapes—is more hazardous even than *The Ghost Sonata*, because the author has not stated its supernatural character quite as firmly. Max Reinhardt's stage version stressed the play's surrealist character, and has secured for it its greatest success to date.

The Last Knight
(*Siste riddaren*, 1908)

The Dramatic Theater in Stockholm proposed to celebrate Stringberg's sixtieth birthday with the première of a new Strindberg play. What could have been more natural, then, than to fill a gap in his brilliant series of plays from Swedish history by writing a nonpolemical play about Sten Sture, the friendly "last knight"—and to do so in a style conventional enough to convert those who felt that Strindberg had become utterly confused? Accordingly, in ten days in the latter part of August of 1908, he wrote the five-act play *The Last Knight*.

The drama describes Sten Sture's conflicts with the Danes and their spokesman, and above all with Gustav Trolle, the icy Machiavellian despot and archbishop. In the first act, Sten Sture appears as the newly elected Regent, gentle and conciliatory; in the second act, Trolle enters as his antagonist; in the superb third act, Trolle scorns Sten Sture's attempts to bring about a reconciliation; in the fourth act, the bishop's castle is taken by assault; and in the fifth act we find Sten Sture on his bier in Stockholm Castle, which is being besieged by Trolle and King Christian.

The structure is rather uneven in the first act, which swarms with minor characters; the action tightens in the second act and reaches its peak in the third, when Sture and Trolle confront each other in the sacristy of Uppsala Cathedral. The two last acts show signs of the difficulties the author had in fusing historical fact with dramatic structure.

ABU CASEM'S SLIPPERS
(*Abu Casems tofflor*, 1908)

When Strindberg moved in 1908 into the last apartment he was ever to occupy, the "blue tower," his landlady Mrs. Falkner had spread for him a table cloth with an oriental design. Strindberg interpreted it as "a welcoming present of the powers," and began to put his mind to writing a play in an oriental setting.

The play tells how Abu Casem's old slippers always find their way back to their owner, whether he throws them in the river or buries them in the ground. However, after the first act the love story of Prince Guri and beautiful Suleika take up so much room that the slippers are nearly forgotten. The whole thing is filled with sunshine, but presented rather mechanically; nevertheless, on the stage it has its charm.

THE REGENT
(*Riksföreståndaren*, 1908)

On September 23, 1908 Strindberg informed his publisher that he had written a sequel to *The Last Knight*: "The second part of the trilogy is finished under the title *The Regent*, stronger than the *Knight*, and very strict in form, like *Damascus I*."

In *The Regent*, we meet the same stage settings as in *The Last Knight*, but in reverse order. Christian has had his blood bath, Gustav Trolle suffers pangs of conscience in Stockholm Castle, and the avenger Gustav Eriksson is approaching. Now from a distance and now close by, we follow the negotiations between Eriksson and Trolle, Bishop Brask, and others, until that midsummer of 1523 when Eriksson, as Gustav Vasa, makes his regal entry into Stockholm.

Strindberg loved variety: after the soft Magnus in *The Folkung Saga*, he created the vigorous Gustav Vasa; after the colorless, conventional Engelbrekt, the brazenly unconventional Christina; after the gentle Sten Sture, the impetuous Gustav Eriksson. As a popular historical drama, *The Regent* has outstanding qualities: down-to-earth dialogue, a popular hero, a central motif of powerful appeal. But it lacks depth of characterization.

THE EARL OF BJÄLBO
(*Bjälbo Jarlen*, 1908)

The third five-act play drawn from Swedish history which Strindberg wrote in the fall of 1908 is more personal in color than its two predecessors. Strindberg describes how the aging Earl Birger sets out to secure power over the entire North by cunning, force, and political marriages, and how he is foiled by fate and by men, until in the end he must surrender his power even in Sweden itself, and settles down on the Isle of Visingsö as a kind of pensioner (just as Strindberg himself dreamed at times of withdrawing to that island, far from all literary feuds and public attention).

"When I wrote *The Earl of Bjälbo*," the author

said in an open letter to the Intimate Theater, "I proceeded as usual. . . . I made the principal characters alive by giving them the blood and nerves of my own life. Thus they became my own, and are of my own substance." The drama contains occasional scenes that are very effective, especially in the final act when Prince Magnus in a surprise move wrests the power from his father the Earl. Here is a final manifestation of Strindberg's special forte: the confrontation of men of power.

Despite the evident pains which Strindberg took to cast his rich material into a drama, the impression remains that he should have proceeded more thoroughly. In the same measure as he takes distance from his characters and treats them as despicable vermin, he puts a distance between them and his audience.

THE BLACK GLOVE
(*Svarta Handsken*, 1909)

At the end of September 1908, Strindberg was working on a Christmas play, which he planned to call *Yule* (*Jul*), but never finished. Instead, toward the end of November, he started on a "lyrical fantasy" which he completed at New Year's 1909 as opus five of the chamber plays; it was entitled *The Black Glove*.

The Black Glove is as fresh and personal a play as *Abu Casem* is impersonal. Its lyrical warmth bears witness to the author's inner life of the emotions which, despite his sixty years, had remained enviably youthful. In a large apartment building there live, among others, a young woman, an octogenarian custodian, a friendly doorman—and also Santa Claus, who does not really belong there. When Christmas approaches, the Christmas angel appears, in white garments and with glittering stars in his hair. The young woman is beautiful but malicious. She has lost a beautiful ring, and immediately accuses her honest maid of theft. In general, she is not interested in making friends, nor does Christmas mean anything to her. The Christmas angel and Santa Claus decide to teach her a lesson. They kidnap her beloved little daughter, and return the child only after the woman has been purified and feels repentance. The lost ring is found in a black glove which she had mislaid, and which the custodian has found. Only now can she celebrate her Christmas in humility and gratitude.

Here, as in earlier plays, an apartment house plays the principal role. The grizzled Strindberg himself was again the new tenant who had to learn the evil secrets of the building. But it was also the same building in which the young actress Fanny Falkner lived, Strindberg's last love. It was the "blue tower," as he had dubbed it, partly because of the blue trademark on the paperbags of the grocery on the ground floor. Today, Strindberg's apartment in the building serves as Strindberg Museum.

THE GREAT HIGHWAY
(*Stora landsvägen*, 1909)

This, Strindberg's final drama, was written in the spring of 1909. The lonely and unsociable author, who barricaded himself inside the "blue tower" behind lock and bolt, and answered the doorbell only on a prearranged signal, felt the urge to formulate his synthesis of life once more—perhaps for the last time—with that lofty wisdom with which the critics of his chamber plays refused to credit him. He also wanted to give the Swedish nation an explication of the state of his mind—to show that he was a forlorn and solitary man, much troubled in his conscience, despite everything. The dramatic form of a journey was eminently suited to his purpose. He could put himself at the play's center without artifice, and could add or subtract scenes at will, according to the number of issues he wished to raise with himself and the world.

At the play's beginning, Strindberg's alter ego, the Hunter, is engaged in an arduous journey high up in the Alps. He has lost his soul among the people of the valley below, and wants to find it again in the solemn temple stillness of eternal snow. But the earth is beautiful, and he finds it hard to leave it. Despite his resolve "to be only an on-looker," he soon finds himself drawn once more into dramatic events on earth. In the Forest of Lies he learns to his amazement how convincingly men can lie; next, in the neighboring Village of the Asses, he becomes embroiled in a contest between two asinine authors. One of the two has written the tragedy *Potamogeton*, the other has composed a memorial address to Charlemagne, "destroyer of the land." The latter, in addition, is married to a woman who has a literary salon—from which the Hunter, however, manages to escape. In the city of Thofeth (Stockholm) he meets, among other characters, a photographer who threatens to take his picture, a Japanese from Hiroshima who intends to commit suicide, and Möller, the murderer who has given the Hunter's daughter a bad upbringing. After defiling the ashes of a conquered enemy in the crematorium, the Hunter lives a nostalgic summer idyl with his daughter, back in the days when she was still a small child. Finally, he enters a dark forest, and there, in a pointed conversation with a blind woman, he defends his life's work and himself, the "advocate of what alone is true, opponent of idol worship" and architect of the "Theater House" in Thofeth. The frivolous tone of the satirical passages subsides, and the piece culminates in a monologue that is profoundly moving.

The Great Highway is a dramatic poem with unexpected and at times astounding twists and turns, a curious mixture of chamber play, satire, fairy play, and lyrical self-revelation. The sequences of the "wander-drama in seven stages" offer an extremely revealing picture of Strindberg's last years, just before he was taken from Stockholm, along The Great Highway, to the New Cemetery, his eighth and final station. The more he had isolated himself, tormented by the thought of Anne-Marie and Harriet Bosse, and harrowed by the noise of his fame and by the hatred which his novel Black Banners had engendered, the more distrustful and hostile he had become toward the world around him.

During his *Inferno* period, when he had discovered the great error that he (and his age) had committed by bowing to materialism, he had wanted above all "to be mad." But now he no longer wanted to forget—now judgment was to be pronounced upon the unjust! "The seals are broken, the books are being opened!" The judge is as unforgiving as the God of the Old Testament, and not a Christian. True, he had once been an "evangelist," but now he had ceased "to preach, in order not to be hypocritical!"

Strindberg's last drama, though inspired, lacks unity. The work is full of whimsicalities, and of allusions which posterity can hardly be expected to appreciate. It has a sheen of deep humanity, but the symbolism is inadequate. Despite his bitterness, despite his nostalgia, the aging author is unable to deny that the earth is of entrancing beauty, and that woman's love and children's laughter still bring him happiness. "For there is happiness, beyond all doubt/but short as a flash of light,/like sunshine and vine blossoms—/*one* flower and *one* day,/and then it is over!"

STRINDBERG'S WORK ON STAGE

Strindberg's plays have been performed in virtually every country in the world where there is a theater. A complete review of the history of his work would fill a substantial tome. We therefore limit ourselves to the premières and other performances that are in some way unusual, especially those in Scandinavia and Germany. The fifty-six plays listed here are arranged in chronological sequence according to the dates within parentheses.

In Rome (*I Rom*, 1870)
Première: September 13, 1870, at the Dramatic Theater in Stockholm. Eleven performances.

The Outlaw (*Den Fredlöse*, 1871)
Première: October 16, 1871, at the Dramatic Theater in Stockholm. First German performance in May, 1902, at the Little Theater in Berlin. Stage direction: Max Reinhardt. Leading role: Emanuel Reicher.

MASTER OLOF (*Mäster Olof*, 1872–1877)
Première of the prose version: December 30, 1881 at the New Theater in Stockholm. Première of the poetic version: March 15, 1890 at the Dramatic Theater in Stockholm. First German performance on September 22, 1916 at the *Volksbühne* in Berlin. Title role: Bruno Decarli.

THE SECRET OF THE GUILD
(*Gillets hemlighet*, 1880)

Première: May 3, 1880 at the Dramatic Theater in Stockholm. First German performance: January 23, 1903 at the Schiller Theater in Berlin.

LUCKY PER'S JOURNEY
(*Lycko-Pers resa*, 1882)

Première: December 2, 1883 at the New Theater in Stockholm. Damned by the press, received enthusiastically by the public. Seventy-six performances. First German performance: Spring, 1921, in Frankfurt-am-Main.

SIR BENGT'S WIFE
(*Herr Bengts hustru*, 1882)

Première: November 25, 1882 at the New Theater in Stockholm. First German performance at the *Schauspielhaus* in Cologne. Title role: Bertha Neuhoff.

COMRADES (*Kamraterna*, 1887)

Première: October 24, 1905 at the Comedy in Vienna with Josef Jarno (Axel), Angela Helm (Bertha), and Gisels Timony (Abel). First Swedish performance: May 17, 1910 at the Intimate Theater in Stockholm.

The Father (*Fadren*, 1887)

Première: November 14, 1887 at the Casino Theater in Copenhagen. Stage direction: Hans Riber Hunderup. Consultant: Georg Brandes(!). As a precaution, this daring presentation was offered on the same bill with the farce *An Excursion to Marienlyst*. After eleven performances, the theater went bankrupt. First German performance, sponsored by The Free Stage (*Die Freie Bühne*): December 12, 1890 at the Lessing Theater in Berlin. Title role: Emanuel Reicher. First Swedish performance: January 12, 1888 at the New Theater in Stockholm. A Turkish group performed the play in Cairo in 1928. While the leading characters wore European dress, the Pastor (now a Moslem) appeared in a turban, and even sat with crossed legs on a sofa smoking his water pipe. The nurse was costumed as a female harem slave.

Miss Julie (*Fröken Julie*, 1888)

Because of difficulties with censorship, the première took place in a private showing of the Students' Association, on March 14, 1889 in Copenhagen, with Strindberg's wife Siri von Essen in the title role. First German performance, sponsored by The Free Stage, in Berlin at the Residence Theater, on April 3, 1892, with Rosa Bertens and Rudolf Rittner. The protests of the public were so violent that there was no second performance. First Swedish performance: fall of 1904, in the Great Guild Hall in Uppsala, as a private showing. (An even more private showing took place in the summer of 1908, at the Intimate Theater in Stockholm, before two interested spectators—George Bernard Shaw and August Strindberg.) The staging by Alf Sjöberg on January 23, 1949 at the Dramatic Theater marks an important point in theatrical history, since it presented the in a certain sense *first complete* performance, restoring to the text all of Strindberg's more vigorous and earthy expressions which the publisher, Seligman, had deleted. The performance with Inga Tidblad (Miss Julie), Ulf Palme (Jean), and Märta Dorff (Kristin), achieved great psychological impact with the aid of its superbly developed stage sets, and became world-famous through traveling engagements of the troupe which took them to Norway, Helsinki, Paris, and Vienna.

CREDITORS (*Fordringsägare*, 1888)
Première: March 9, 1889 at the Dagmar Theater in Copenhagen, sponsored by the "Strindberg Experimental Theater," with the writer Gustav Wied in the role of Adolf. First Swedish performance on March 25, 1890 in a matinée at the Swedish Theater in Stockholm. First German performance: January 22, 1893 as "Benefit Matinée" at the Residence Theater in Berlin. Cast: Rosa Bertens (Tekla), Rudolf Rittner (Adolf), and Josef Jarno (Gustav). On April 24, 1895 the "Society for Modern Life," in Munich, under the sponsorship of The Free Stage, offered a performance at a private home before an audience of fifty. The dramatist Julius Schaumberger played Gustav, Max Halve took the role of Adolf. The writer Oskar Panizza was the prompter. On the day after the performance, Panizza was sentenced to a year's imprisonment for his satire "The Love Council."

THE STRONGER (*Den starkara*, 1889)
Première: March 9, 1889 at the Dagmar Theater in

Copenhagen. First Swedish performance: March 16, 1889 in Malmö, together with *Pariah* and *Creditors*. First German performance, together with *The Link*, on March 11, 1902 at the Little Theater in Berlin, with Rosa Bertens (Mrs. X) and Gertrud Eysoldt (Miss Y), under the direction of Max Reinhardt.

PARIAH (*Paria*, 1889)

Première: March 9, 1889 at the Dagmar Theater in Copenhagen. First Swedish performance: March 16, 1889 in Malmö, together with the one-act play *The Stronger* (1889). First German performance: spring of 1900, at the Residence Theater in Berlin. In 1908, *Pariah* was performed in Esperanto, jointly with *Miss Julie*, in Dresden, Germany. In 1936, the play was performed in Reykjavik (Iceland); the cast included August Falck, former director of the Intimate Theater of Stockholm, and the Dean of the Stockholm Academy, Professor Sven Tunberg.

HEMSÖ FOLK (*Hemsöborna*, 1889)

Première: May 29, 1889 at the *Tiergartentheater* in Stockholm. First German performance: March 1906 at the Town Theater in Altona.

SIMOOM (*Samum*, 1889)

Première: March 25, 1908 in a matinée (with *Creditors*) at the Swedish Theater in Stockholm. First German performance: spring 1905 at the Lobe Theater in Breslau.

THE KEYS OF THE KINGDOM OF HEAVEN (*Himmelrikets nycklar*, 1892)

Première: fall of 1926, at the Stage in Bad Godesberg. Stage direction: Martin Ullrich. First semiprofessional open-air performance in Sweden, June 21, 1962 at Uppsala Castle. Stage direction: Stig Ossian Ericsson. First Swedish performance: October 13, 1967 at the Town Theater in Norrköping under the direction of Johan Falck.

THE FIRST WARNING
(*Första varningen*, 1892)

Première: January 22, 1893 as "Benefit Matinée" (together with *Creditors*) at the Residence Theater in Berlin. First Swedish performance: spring 1907, in Julia Håkansson's tour.

DEBIT AND CREDIT
(*Debet och kredit*, 1892)

Première: May 13, 1900 at the Residence Theater in Berlin. First Swedish performance: August 31, 1915 at the Dramatic Theater in Stockholm, in the framework of a "Strindberg Week."

FACING DEATH (*Inför döden*, 1892)

Première: January 22, 1893 as "Benefit Matinée" (together with *Creditors* and *The First Warning*) at the Residence Theater in Berlin. First Swedish performance: spring 1907, on a tour.

MOTHERLOVE (*Moderskärlek*, 1892)

Première: 1894, during the Massthaler tour (with the subtitle *A Summer Dream*). First Swedish performance: fall 1909, at the Theater in Uppsala, with Maria Schildknecht as the Mother.

PLAYING WITH FIRE
(*Leka med elden*, 1892)

Première: December 1893, at the Lessing Theater

in Berlin. First Swedish performance: spring 1907, on the occasion of a soirée in Stockholm. Mauritz Stiller, the discoverer of Greta Garbo, played the Friend. In the spring of 1922, Maria Orska gave a guest performance at the Blanche Theater in Stockholm, in the role of Kerstin.

THE LINK (*Bandet*, 1892)

Première: March 11, 1902 at the Little Theater in Berlin. Stage direction: Max Reinhardt. Cast: Emanuel Reicher, Rosa Bertens, and others. First Swedish performance: January 31, 1908 at the Intimate Theater in Stockholm.

TO DAMASCUS, PART I
(*Till Damaskus I*, 1898)

Première: November 19, 1900 at the Dramatic Theater in Stockholm, under the direction of Emil Grandinson, with August Palme (The Unknown) and Harriet Bosse (the Lady). First German performance: April 27, 1914 at the Lessing Theater in Berlin, with Friedrich Kaissler and Lina Lossen. On February 27, 1937, Olof Molander's epoch-making staging of the play at the Dramatic Theater, with Lars Hanson as a congenial Unknown, contributed to radical changes in the interpretation of Strindberg on the Swedish stage.

TO DAMASCUS, PART II
(*Till Damaskus II*, 1898)

Première: June 9, 1916 (together with *Part III*, in a performance lasting four and one-half hours, in a text adapted by Friedrich Kaissler) at the Chamber Play Theater in Munich. First Swedish performance of *Part II*: December 9, 1924 at the Lorensberg Theater in Göteborg. First Swedish performance of *Parts II* and *III* at one sitting: spring 1944, at the Dramatic Theater in Stockholm, under the direction of Olof Molander.

To Damascus, Part III
(*Till Damaskus III*, 1901)

Première: June 9, 1916 (together with *Part II*, in a performance lasting four and one-half hours, in a text adapted by Friedrich Kaissler), at the Chamber Play Theater in Munich. First Swedish performance of *Part III* alone: November 16, 1922 at the Lorensberg Theater in Göteborg under the direction of Knut Ström. In 1926, Per Lindberg presented his expressionistic staging at the Concert Hall Theater in Stockholm.

Advent (1898)

Première: December 28, 1915 at the Chamber Play Theater in Munich. First Swedish performance: January 22, 1926 at the Dramatic Theater in Stockholm. Direction: Olof Molander.

There Are Crimes and Crimes
(*Brott och brott*, 1899)

Première: February 26, 1900 at the Dramatic Theaater in Stockholm. First German performance: August 1900 at the New Summer Theater in Breslau. Max Reinhardt's presentation at the Little Theater in Berlin had its first performance on October 13, 1902, and is considered the event by which Strindberg became definitively established on the German stage. Emanuel Reicher played Maurice, Gertrud Eysoldt, Henriette.

The Folkung Saga
(*Folkungasagan*, 1899)

Première: January 25, 1901 at the Swedish Theater in Stockholm. First German performance: May 1916 at the Thalia Theater in Hamburg under the direction of Hermann Röbeling.

Gustav Vasa (1899)

Première: October 17, 1899 at the Swedish Theater in Stockholm. Stage direction: Harald Molander. Title role: Emil Hillberg. First German performance: fall 1900 at the Hoftheater in Schwerin.

Erik XIV (1899)

Première: November 30, 1899 at the Swedish Theater in Stockholm, under the direction of Harald Molander. Title role: Anders de Wahl. First German performance: November 1902 at the Hoftheater in Schwerin. Evgeni Vakhtangov, in 1921, offered a sensational interpretation in the expressionist manner at the Moscow Art Theater, after years of trials and rehearsals with his ensemble. Vakhtangov shifted the emphasis away from Strindberg's portrayal of Erik's destruction by his fellow kings, and instead laid stress upon the decline and fall of royal power and the triumph of the people. Thanks to this shift, the play could remain in the regular repertory for many years.

Gustav Adolf (1900)

Première: December 4, 1903 at the Berlin Theater. First Swedish performance: June 4, 1912 at the Circus in Stockholm. Strindberg himself had made certain cuts, but died during rehearsals. This first performance was then offered as a memorial presentation.

MIDSUMMER (*Midsommar*, 1900)
Première: April 17, 1901 at the Swedish Theater in Stockholm.

CASPER'S SHROVE TUESDAY
(*Kaspers fet-tisdag*, 1900)
Première: April 16, 1901 at the Dramatic Theater in Stockholm, as a postlude to *Easter*. On May 11, 1961 the play was performed in Korbach (Germany), largely in pantomime, under the title *Kasperle's Happy Graveyard Journey*.

EASTER (*Påsk*, 1900)
Première: March 9, 1901 at the Playhouse in Frankfurt-am-Main, with Gertrud Eysoldt as Eleonora. First Swedish performance: April 4, 1901 at the Dramatic Theater in Stockholm, with Harriet Bosse as Eleonora. However, only the presentation at the Intimate Theater in Stockholm, on April 16, 1908 secured for the play the full success it deserved, and gave the Intimate Theater the record run of all its Strindberg pieces—182 performances. Eleonora was played by Anna Flygare.

THE DANCE OF DEATH (*Dödsdansen*, 1900)
Première: *Part I* on September 29, 1905 at the Old Town Theater in Cologne, *Part II* on September 30 on the same stage. A guest performance of the "August Strindberg Tour" under the direction of Krempiens and Jaffé. In the cast: Elimar Striebeck and Helene Riechers. First Swedish performance of *Part I* on September 8, 1909, *Part II* on October 1, 1909 at the Intimate Theater in Stockholm, with August Falck in the male lead. In the fall of 1912, Max Reinhardt staged both parts at the German

Theater in Berlin, with Paul Wegener and Gertrud Eysoldt. In November of 1915, Reinhardt brought his version to the Royal Theater in Stockholm, as a guest performance—a triumphant success for Paul Wegener in the role of the Captain.

THE BRIDAL CROWN (*Kronbruden*, 1901)

Première: April 24, 1906 at the Swedish Theater in Helsinki, with Harriet Bosse as Kersti. Strindberg's daughter Greta played the leading role during a Strindberg tour 1909–10. First German performance: November 5, 1913 at the Theater on Königgrätz Street in Berlin, with Irene Triesch in the leading role, Paul Wegener as the Bondsman, and Otto Gebühr as the Nurse.

SWANWHITE (*Svanevit*, 1901)

Première: April 8, 1908 at the Swedish Theater in Helsinki. First German performance, directed by Max Reinhardt, at the Playhouse in Berlin in 1913, with Helene Thimig in the leading role.

CARL XII (1901)

Première: February 13, 1902 at the Dramatic Theater in Stockholm, with August Palme in the title role, omitting the third act—an omission which Strindberg considered a disastrous mistake. First German performance: fall 1922 at the Town Theater in Hanover.

ENGELBREKT (1901)

Première: December 3, 1901 at the Swedish Theater in Stockholm.

CHRISTINA (*Kristina*, 1901)

Première: March 27, 1908 at the Intimate Theater in Stockholm, with Manda Björling in the title role. August Falck, who was the stage director, used nothing but velvet draperies for his stage set. The presentation ended as a notable failure in the history of drama. First performance in the German language: October 1910, in Vienna, at the Theater in der Josefstadt, with Emmy Schroth.

A DREAM PLAY (*Ett drömspel*, 1901)

Première: April 17, 1907 at the Swedish Theater in Stockholm, with Harriet Bosse as Indra's Daughter. Direction: Victor Castegren. First German performance: March 17, 1916 at the Theater on König-grätz Street, in Berlin, with Irene Triesch. The expressionistic stage decor was done by Svend Gade. On October 28, 1921, the curtain of the Dramatic Theater in Stockholm rose for Max Reinhardt's sensational guest performance.

GUSTAV III (1902)

Première: January 25, 1916 at the new Intimate Theater in Stockholm, with Lars Hanson in the title role. First German performance: fall 1924 at the Landestheater in Stuttgart. Direction: Wolfgang Hoffman-Harnisch.

THE HOLLANDER (*Holländaren*, 1902)

Première: April 5, 1923 at the Lorensberg Theater in Göteborg. First German performance, same year, in Jena.

THE NIGHTINGALE IN WITTENBERG
(*Näktergalen i Wittenberg*, 1903)

Première: December 5, 1914 at the German Art

Theater in Berlin, with Friedrich Kaissler as Luther. First Swedish performance: January 26, 1917 at the Swedish Theater in Stockholm.

THROUGH THE WILDERNESS TO
THE PROMISED LAND, OR MOSES
(*Genom öknar till arvland, eller Moses*, 1903)

Première: fall 1922, at the Town Theater in Hanover.

HELLAS, OR SOCRATES
(*Hellas, eller Sokrates*, 1903)

Première: fall 1922 at the Town Theater in Hanover.

THE LAMB AND THE WILD BEAST,
OR CHRIST
(*Lammet och vilddjuret, eller Kristus*, 1903)

Première: fall 1922 at the Town Theater in Hanover. On September 28, 1929 the play was performed in St. George's Church in Hamburg, the first Strindberg play to be shown in a church. Direction: Verner Arpe.

THE THUNDERSTORM (*Oväder*, 1907)

Première: December 30, 1909 at the Intimate Theater in Stockholm. First German performance: 1910, at the Artists' Theater in Berlin.

AFTER THE FIRE (*Brända tomten*, 1907)

Première: December 5, 1907 at the Intimate Theater in Stockholm. First German performance: 1910, at the Artists' Theater in Berlin.

THE GHOST SONATA (*Spöksonaten*, 1907)
Première: January 21, 1908 at the Intimate Theater in Stockholm. First German performance: October 17, 1916 at the Chamber Play Theater in Berlin, under the direction of Max Reinhardt. The role of Hummel was realized by Paul Wegener who, by his performance, contributed substantially to the play's international success. Max Reinhardt had the opportunity to show his presentation in Sweden as well, during 1916 and 1917; the excellent reviews of these performances underlined that the manner in which Strindberg's work was being presented in Germany might well serve as a model for the Swedish stage. Olof Molander had meanwhile abandoned "romantic expressionism." In the fall of 1942, he added to his outstanding Strindberg interpretations an altogether remarkable and wholly original presentation of *The Ghost Sonata*. It was performed at the Intimate Theater, with Lars Hanson as Hummel and Märta Ekström as the Mummy.

THE PELICAN (*Pelikanen*, 1907)
Première: November 26, 1907, on the occasion of the opening of the Intimate Theater in Stockholm. First performance in German: November 1908, in Vienna (Vienna Chamber Play evenings). *The Pelican* gave to Max Reinhardt and his ensemble a further opportunity, during his 1920 guest tour in Göteborg and Stockholm, to demonstrate to their Swedish colleagues the full stage potential of Strindberg's chamber plays. Agnes Straub as the Mother, Helene Thimig as the Daughter, Ernst Deutsch as the Son, and Heinrich George as the Son-in-law left unforgettable impressions.

THE LAST KNIGHT (*Siste riddaren*, 1908)
Première: January 22, 1909 at the Dramatic Theater in Stockholm. Direction: Emil Grandinson. First German performance: fall 1927 at the State Playhouse in Dresden. Paul Hoffman in the title role.

ABU CASEM'S SLIPPERS
(*Abu Casems tofflor*, 1908)
Première: December 28, 1908 in Gävle (Sweden), on the occasion of Karin Swanström's tour.

THE REGENT (*Riksföreståndaren*, 1908)
Première: January 31, 1911 at the Dramatic Theater in Stockholm. First German performance: September 25, 1928 at the State Theater, Gotha, under the title *Der Befreier*.

THE EARL OF BJÄLBO
(*Bjälbo-Jarlen*, 1908)
Première: March 26, 1909 at the Swedish Theater in Stockholm. First German performance: fall 1926, at the Old Town Theater in Nuremberg, under the title *Der Jarl*.

THE BLACK GLOVE
(*Svarta handsken*, 1909)
Première: Christmas of 1909, during a tour of the Swedish provinces, with Greta Strindberg as the Woman. First German performance: spring 1918 at the Chamber Playhouse in Berlin, under the title *Der Handschuh* (*Fröhliche Weihnacht*).

THE GREAT HIGHWAY
(*Stora landsvägen*, 1909)
Première: February 19, 1910 at the Intimate Theater in Stockholm. First German performance: 1923,

in Frankfurt-am-Main. In the hundredth anniversary year of Strindberg's birth, on January 21, 1949,
the Dramatic Theater in Stockholm offered Olof
Molander's outstanding staging, with Lars Hanson
as the Hunter. This presentation was also shown on
May 10, 1949 at the National Theater in Oslo.

BIBLIOGRAPHY

Selected English Translations of the Plays

The Chamber Plays. Translated by Evert Sprinchorn, Seabury Quinn, Jr., and Kenneth Peter-
sen. New York: E. P. Dutton, 1962.

Eight Expressionist Plays. Tranlated by Arvid Paulson. New York: Bantam Books, 1965.

Five Plays of Strindberg. Translated by Elizabeth
Sprigge. Garden City, N.Y.: Doubleday, 1960.

Gustav Adolf. Translated by Walter Johnson.
Seattle: University of Washington Press, 1957.

The Last of the Knights; *The Regent*; *Earl Birger
of Bjälbo*. Translated by Walter Johnson.
Seattle: University of Washington Press, 1956.

The Plays of Strindberg. Vol. 1. Translated by
Michael Meyer. New York: Random House,
1964.

Queen Christina; *Charles XII*; *Gustav III*. Translated by Walter Johnson. Seattle: University
of Washington Press, 1955.

The Saga of the Folkungs; *Engelbrekt*. Translated
by Walter Johnson. Seattle: University of
Washington Press, 1959.

Seven Plays. Translated by Arvid Paulson. New York: Bantam Books, 1960.

Six Plays of Strindberg. Translated by Elizabeth Sprigge. Garden City, N.Y.: Doubleday, 1955.

Strindberg's One-Act Plays. Translated by Arvid Paulson. New York: Washington Square Press, 1969.

The Vasa Trilogy (Master Olof; Gustav Vasa; Erik XIV). Translated by Walter Johnson. Seattle: University of Washington Press, 1959.

OTHER WORKS BY STRINDBERG

Inferno, Alone and Other Writings. Translated by Evert Sprinchorn. Garden City, N.Y.: Doubleday, 1968.

A Madman's Defense. Translated by Evert Sprinchorn. Garden City, N.Y.: Doubleday, 1967.

Open Letters to the Intimate Theater. Translated by Walter Johnson. Seattle: University of Washington Press, 1966.

The Son of a Servant. Translated by Evert Sprinchorn. Garden City, N.Y.: Doubleday, 1966.

SELECTED CRITICISM

Benston, Alice N. "From Naturalism to the Dream Play: A Study of the Evolution of Strindberg's Unique Theatrical Form." *Modern Drama* 7 (February 1965): 382–98.

Bentley, Eric. *The Playwright as Thinker.* Cleveland: World Publishing Company, 1955.

Brustein, Robert. *The Theatre of Revolt.* Boston: Little, Brown, 1964.

Collis, John Stewart. *Marriage and Genius: Strindberg and Tolstoy, Studies in Tragi-comedy.* London: Cassell, 1963.

Dahlström, Carl. *Strindberg's Dramatic Expressionism.* 2nd. ed. New York: Benjamin Blom, 1965.

Freedman, Morris. "Strindberg's Positive Nihilism." *Drama Survey* 2 (Fall 1963): 288–96.

Johnson, Walter. *Strindberg and the Historical Drama.* Seattle: University of Washington Press, 1963.

Kaufmann, R. J. "Strindberg: The Absence of Irony." *Drama Survey* 3 (Fall 1964): 463–76.

Klaf, Franklin S. *Strindberg: The Origin of Psychology in Modern Drama.* New York: Citadel Press, 1963.

Lamm, Martin. "Strindberg and the Theatre." *Tulane Drama Review* 6 (November 1961): 132–39.

Lucas, F. L. *The Drama of Ibsen and Strindberg.* London: Cassell, 1962.

McGill, Vivian. *August Strindberg: The Bedeviled Viking.* New York: Russell & Russell, 1965.

Mortensen, Brita, and Downs, Brian. *Strindberg: An Introduction to His Life and Work.* Cambridge: Cambridge University Press, 1949.

Sprinchorn, Evert. "Strindberg and the Greater Naturalism." *Drama Review* 13 (Winter 1968): 119–29.

Valency, Maurice. *The Flower and the Castle: An Introduction to Modern Drama.* New York: Macmillan, 1963.

World Theatre (Strindberg issue). 10 (Spring 1962): 3–79.

INDEX